T0194266

GOD,
DO YOU
REALLY
CARE?

GOD,
DO YOU
REALLY
CARE?

TONY EVANS

MULTNOMAH
BOOKS

CONTENTS

God, Do You Really Care...

INTRODUCTION

On Monday, August 29, 2005, a hurricane named Katrina smashed and screamed her way into national history.

An extremely powerful category 4 storm, she barreled out of the Gulf of Mexico and tore her way through the Gulf Coast, laying waste to coastal cities in Louisiana, Mississippi, and Alabama, and virtually destroying the great historical city of New Orleans.

In her wake, the monster hurricane left mind-numbing destruction, death, and suffering. Over 1,100 people lost their lives, and several hundred thousand lost their homes—and everything else that had been a part of their lives before the storm.

It has been called the worst natural disaster in our nation's history.

In addition to the pictures of death and destruction, news reports in the days and weeks following this horrific event showed a shocked world heartrending pictures of human pain and deprivation. People grieving over the loss of loved ones, people walking around in a confused stupor because they had nowhere to go, and people wondering what their futures held—these were just a few of the unforgettable images we saw on our television screens. On more than one occasion, victims and veteran journalists alike broke down in front of the camera over the horror of what was happening.

Most viewers responded to the storm with sadness and sympathy. It was difficult not to be moved, even to the point of tears, at the plight of the men, women, and children who survived Katrina. We knew their suffering wouldn't end overnight, or even in a few weeks or months. We knew that the lives of many people caught up in the storm's path of devastation would never be the same.

As a minister of the gospel of Jesus Christ, I'm often asked after events like this whether God really cares. Does He care when people are sick, injured, and dying? Does He care when they grieve over death—the death of loved ones, the death of their own goals and dreams? Does God concern Himself when people, even people who didn't have much to begin with, lose everything? Is He moved when men and women are confused and lost, picking through the rubble and devastation of their lives?

Why would God allow such suffering? Could He really be the

loving heavenly Father He's been made out to be? Doesn't He seem more like a passive bystander to our pain sometimes? Truth be told, it can sometimes look—within human reasoning anyway—as though God doesn't really care all that much that people are suffering.

I can easily understand thoughts like these boiling to the surface in the hearts of those who don't know God, and who are outside the faith. But I also hear variations of these same questions from the mouths of Bible-believing Christians. In fact, I would go so far as to say that any believer—even the most devoted—who tells you that he or she has never looked at life and its sorrows and wondered whether God cared isn't being truthful.

Yes, we know the Bible says that God so loved the world that He sent His one and only Son so that we could have eternal life. We know that. But there are times, perhaps, when we question whether He's really all that interested in our pain, suffering, and confusion *in the here and now*.

Of course none of this is new. As we will see, men and women have questioned God since the beginning of time, even asking Him point blank if He was even concerned about what was happening to them:

Arouse Yourself, why do You sleep, O Lord?
    Awake, do not reject us forever.
Why do You hide Your face
    And forget our affliction and our oppression?

For our soul has sunk down into the dust;

Our body cleaves to the earth.

PSALM 44:23–25

It's not known for sure who wrote this psalm or when, but a few things appear certain: First, the psalmist and his people were enduring some heartbreaking and difficult times, times when they suffered under the affliction and oppression of their enemies. Second, the psalmist himself wondered if God was paying attention to His people's plight.

Hurricane Katrina was far from the first time people have had to endure disaster, hardship, and sorrow, and you can be sure it won't be the last. We live in a fallen world where wars, storms, earthquakes, tsunamis, and other calamities will always be a part of the human landscape—at least until the promised return of Jesus.

Each of us at different points in our lives will find ourselves in a position where we'll wonder if God cares personally about our situation. Sickness, fear, confusion, death, doubt, disappointment—all are common to men and women everywhere. In the midst of these events, we all need the answer to one key question: Does God care when we hurt? I've written this book to answer you unequivocally: *Yes, He cares!*

I want to show you that God is not only aware when we're caught up in the difficulties of life, but that He also has a plan to meet us and speak to us in those times of trial, strengthening us and teaching us all along the way. But I also want to show you that although He cares, God doesn't always resolve our difficulties in the way we expect Him to.

He *will* answer the heart-cries of His loved ones. But He will do it in His own time and His own way for His own good purposes.

I've based this book on a passage of Scripture that is very near and dear to me. John 11 tells the story of Jesus raising His friend Lazarus from the dead, as well as the events leading up to and following that event. You may be quite familiar with the fact that Jesus raised Lazarus, but in this book I want to take a closer look at these events and what they tell us about how much God cares, and how He may choose to intervene during seasons of difficulty in this life.

We will walk through this amazing story several times—rewinding the tape here and there to focus on some fascinating aspects you might not have considered before. So read on, and you will find your answer to the question, *God, do you really care...?*

God, Do You Really Care...
WHEN I'M SICK?

Over the course of my ministry, I've spent time with hundreds of believers, whose bodies have been afflicted by illness and injury. In the wake of those physical setbacks and seasons of pain, I often hear questions like these:

- *If God really loves me, why is He allowing me to suffer this way?*
- *Is God paying attention? What is He going to do for me now that I'm sick?*
- *Where is God when I'm sick and need Him most?*
- *Why doesn't God just step in and heal me?*

When we or a loved one is sick, it's easy to question whether God cares because, frankly, it's at those times when it seems He doesn't. In our human thinking, if He was truly concerned about us, He wouldn't allow us to go on suffering that way.

So does God care when we are sick? Absolutely! In fact, I'd say that when we are suffering—be it from physical illness or any other painful situation—He expresses His tender care for us more than ever.

The Bible is filled with declarations of God's loving, caring heart for those who suffer. But I want to focus our attention on an account in which Jesus demonstrates over and over just how much He cares for those He loves. It's the account of the sickness and physical death of a man named Lazarus—and the stunning miracle Jesus performed on his behalf and on the behalf of his sisters, Mary and Martha.

JESUS LOVES ME, YET...

The story of Lazarus begins in the New Testament book of John, chapter 11.

> Now a certain man was sick, Lazarus of Bethany, the vil-
> lage of Mary and her sister Martha. It was the Mary who
> anointed the Lord with ointment, and wiped His feet with

her hair, whose brother Lazarus was sick. So the sisters sent word to Him, saying, "Lord, behold, he whom You love is sick."

vv. 1 – 3

John, you'll notice, goes out of his way to tell us that Jesus loved Lazarus. This wasn't just brotherly love for a fellow human being, but a personal, heartfelt love. Jesus loved Lazarus with the love of God, the one and only perfect love—what the Bible calls *agape* love.

Yet Lazarus wasn't just sick; he was gravely ill. In the original language of John's Gospel, the word *sick* refers to a sickness leading to death. In other words, Lazarus was dying.

This demonstrates something we all need to keep in mind: It is possible for Jesus to love us and for us to love Him in return and still get sick—even deathly sick. Not only that, there are times when God allows us to become sick for specific purposes in His great (and often incomprehensible) plan.

We live in a time when some believe that those who love Jesus should never be sick, and that if they do experience illness their faith is enough to repel any affliction that befalls them. It's a nice thought, but that is not a sound reading of God's Word. The Bible gives us several examples of people God loved going through problems of all kinds— including persecution, injury, *and* physical illness.

In the case of Lazarus, someone Jesus loved had fallen deathly ill. And it was a situation that was going to get a lot worse before it got better.

FROM BAD TO WORSE

Faced with a problem beyond their ability to fix, Mary and Martha sent word to Jesus. This is a simple but beautiful example of what prayer really is: taking our problems or situations to the Father through Jesus Christ, and humbly asking Him to provide the remedy we could never provide.

Obviously, Mary and Martha wanted Jesus to come to Bethany right away and heal their brother. To them, it was a simple formula of Jesus' love and their request equaling healing for Lazarus.

But it didn't happen that way.

Jesus did not drop everything He was doing and go to Lazarus immediately, but stayed two more days where He was—in Perea. The Gospels call Perea "the land beyond the Jordan." It was about forty miles from Bethany, which was about two miles east of Jerusalem. Instead, of coming immediately, Jesus sent these words of assurance: "This sickness is not to end in death, but for the glory of God, that the Son of God may be glorified by it" (John 11:4).

Meanwhile, Lazarus didn't get well. In fact, his condition only worsened. And Jesus wouldn't show up in Bethany until it was—in

Mary and Martha's minds anyway—too late. By the time He would arrive, Lazarus would have been dead and buried.

In our human thinking, that doesn't sound very much like a Savior who cared when His close friend became sick, does it? Jesus had already proven over and over that He had the supernatural ability to do something about Lazarus's sickness.

So...He had the ability. He loved Lazarus. He loved Mary and Martha. The sisters had exercised simple faith in asking Him to come. But He did nothing, and their beloved brother was slipping away.

When we are faced with sickness, we tend to believe—probably as Mary and Martha did—that if God truly cared He would step in and do something about it. But it doesn't always happen that way. In fact, our situation may stay the same—or even become worse.

Certainly God has the ability to heal us in an instant, but just as certainly there are many times when He doesn't. *But that doesn't mean He doesn't care*, and Jesus' words for Mary and Martha's messengers demonstrate that fact.

We live in a fallen world corrupted by sin—where sickness, physical death, and heartbreak are part of our lives. But as believers, we never have to view our illness as a "waste of time" or a "worthless experience." In fact, we can be sure that God has allowed our illness for His eternal and spiritual purposes. In light of that biblical truth, we should never ask, "Why me?" in our suffering, but instead, "For what purpose has God allowed this?"

Jesus had already told Mary and Martha that Lazarus's sickness was "for the glory of God." But God uses our physical sicknesses for another eternal purpose, and it's for correction and personal growth in our lives.

DISCIPLINARY SICKNESS

This is so incredibly difficult for us. I believe that one of the biggest weaknesses in the church today is our inability to make spiritual connections between what we're going through physically and what God wants to teach us and do in us through those things.

Yes, our God is a God of love. John tells us that God *is* love.

But He is also a Father who, in His love, corrects His children.

The Bible is very clear that there are times when God uses physical sickness in the lives of His children as a means of discipline or correction. The apostle Paul gives us an example in his first letter to the Corinthian church:

> For he who eats and drinks, eats and drinks judgment to himself if he does not judge the body rightly. For this reason many among you are weak and sick, and a number sleep. But if we judged ourselves rightly, we would not be judged. But when we are judged, we are disciplined by the Lord so that we will not be condemned along with the world.
>
> 1 CORINTHIANS 11:29–32

The Corinthian church had a simple but very serious issue: They were taking communion, the meal commemorating the sacrificial death of Christ, without first addressing personal sin. Because of that, God's hand of discipline was upon them, and many of them suffered physically.

God cares when we are physically sick, but He is even more concerned that our lives be free of sin.

Those of us who are parents know that no matter how much we love our children, there are times when it's necessary for us to go to the "rod of correction." The very same is true of our heavenly Father. He has identified Himself as the God who loves tenderly and compassionately, and His love compels Him to correct us, sometimes using difficulties in our lives, including physical illness.

SICKNESS FOR GOD'S GLORY

While God sometimes allows illness to inflict our bodies in order to correct us, He also has another purpose in mind: to bring Himself glory.

We see an example of that in John's Gospel, just a few chapters before the story of Lazarus. Jesus and the disciples had encountered a man born blind begging near the Temple in Jerusalem. The disciples, who obviously didn't understand that God often had a higher purpose for people's illnesses and disabilities, asked Jesus, "Rabbi, who sinned, this man or his parents, that he would be born blind?" (John 9:2).

Jesus didn't correct the disciples' notion that sin could bring this kind of calamity into a person's life, but instead told them that this man's blindness was part of God's plan to focus the world's attention on the Father and the Son. This, He told them, had nothing to do with anyone's sin, but had happened so that the power of God could be put on display that day.

And that's just what happened! It wasn't long after Jesus healed this blind beggar that news of this miraculous healing began to spread throughout Jerusalem. Some greeted this miracle healing with skepticism, while others were sure this was the same man they had for years seen begging near the Temple.

When the former blind man was brought before the Jewish religious leadership and grilled about what had happened, all he could tell them was, "The man who is called Jesus made clay, and anointed my eyes, and said to me, 'Go to Siloam and wash'; so I went away and washed, and I received sight" (John 9:11).

This beggar's blindness had nothing to do with sin and everything to do with God glorifying Himself before an unbelieving world. The very same is true of Lazarus.

So we find ourselves ill...with some physical affliction in our body. Did God allow it as a correction in our lives to help us grow, or is it solely to bring glory to His name? That's an important question. When we don't know which it is, it's difficult for us to pray and act rightly toward our situation—just as a doctor would find it difficult to prescribe a right treatment for a physical problem without a careful diagnosis.

But how can we know the difference?

We have to ask Him.

It's simply a matter of asking God for the answer, then waiting for a personal word from Him.

A PERSONAL WORD

Jesus didn't give Mary and Martha the immediate solution they had asked in faith to receive. But He didn't remain silent about it either. He didn't leave His friends "twisting in the wind."

Jesus demonstrated how much He cared about Mary and Martha—as well as their sick brother—when He gave them something God wants to give each of us today: a personal word.

When Jesus told these ladies, "This sickness is not unto death, but for the glory of God, that the Son of God may be glorified by it," He wasn't talking about sickness in general. Jesus started out His promise to Mary and Martha with the phrase "*This* sickness," meaning that He was speaking specifically to *them* and to *their* situation.

The same is true for us today.

When you are sick and hurting, it's vitally important to hear what God has to say to you in the midst of your situation. In other words, you need to hear a personal word from God. While many Christians today hear the Word *of* God, I wonder how many really hear a word *from* God. By that I mean that while they may know the Bible well and are fully aware of God's promises, they have never personalized it, never taken the time to read and study it, and then ask God, "What are you saying to *me personally* through Your Word?"

It has been said that the Bible is God's love letter to a fallen world. But it's much more than that. It's His love letter to each and every one of us personally and individually. All we need to do is make it *our* personal message from Him.

Every Sunday, I stand up in front of our church and deliver a sermon based on the Word of God. You might come to visit us someday. (I hope you do. You would be welcome.) If you walked through the doors of Oak Cliff Bible Fellowship Church in Dallas, Texas, on most any given Sunday, you would hear my sermon to the whole congregation. But what if you and I were to go out to coffee, and across that little table, I gave you the essence of my message face-to-face?

That's a different dynamic, isn't it? Then it would become a personal message to you and you alone.

That is very much how God speaks to us personally through His Word. When we simply read it and understand it, it is still the

Word of God to us; but when you read it as a personal God-to-you message (and it is), then you receive a personalized word from Him.

You need to have a passion to hear, know, and understand the written Word of God because that is how you can hear a word *from* God. If you don't have the Word of God written in your mind and heart, you're hindered from hearing what He wants to say to you in your suffering. But when you know the Word of God, you can hear the voice of the Holy Spirit more clearly—at the very time when you so desperately long for answers.

Many of us in our personal Bible studies take fluorescent yellow pens and highlight particular verses or passages of Scripture so that they will "jump out at us" later on. But the Holy Spirit goes much further than that, actually taking a verse or passage we read and making it jump off the page and into our minds and hearts.

This is why it's so important for us to go to the Scriptures regularly—and especially when we need more than ever to hear from God. When we make it our habit to consistently and regularly devote ourselves to the reading and studying of the Bible, we will have more confidence that we're truly hearing God's personal word to us.

But what about those times when we're so sick or weak or in despair that we have difficulty even reaching out to God and asking for a personal word? Then we can receive yet another great gift of our God: the overflow and blessing of God's love and communication to brothers and sisters who daily walk with Him.

CARING FOR US THROUGH OTHERS

Even though Lazarus was sick to the point of physical death, he wasn't alone in his illness. On the contrary, he faced his sickness within the context of a caring earthly family and a caring spiritual family—an earthly family because his sisters were with him and a spiritual family because they loved Jesus.

Lazarus didn't need to send for his Friend and Lord in his illness; Mary and Martha took care of that. And the message they sent to Jesus in Perea was based on two things: their love for their brother...and their belief that Jesus loved them and could do something about it.

How do we know these things about Mary and Martha?

The answer to that is found in John 11:2, which tells us something about Mary that at first might escape our attention. She is specifically described as the one who "anointed the Lord with ointment, and wiped His feet with her hair."

John wrote his Gospel several decades after Jesus' death and resurrection, and when he tells us that Mary was the one who had anointed Jesus with oil, he was referring to an incident recorded one chapter later, just days before Jesus would finally enter into Jerusalem for the final time.

In the culture of that time and place, anointing someone's feet was an outward expression of adoration, even worship. When Mary anointed Jesus' feet, she was expressing her love and adoration, an act He not only allowed but encouraged (see John 12:7–8). This shows us something about Mary's relationship with Jesus: She had a special connection with Him, and she didn't care what others thought as she openly worshiped Him.

When we are sick or hurting and can't make a "prayer connection" with God, He uses others to demonstrate how much He cares for us. It is during those times that we need to be close to somebody who knows how to get close to Jesus, someone who regularly sits at His feet and worships Him.

That is what the apostle James was referring to when he wrote:

> Is anyone among you sick? Then he must call for the elders of the church and they are to pray over him, anointing him with oil in the name of the Lord; and the prayer offered in faith will restore the one who is sick, and the Lord will raise him up, and if he has committed sins, they will be forgiven him.
>
> J A M E S   5 : 1 4 – 1 5

Why should we call the elders to pray for us? Because when we are sick, it may be difficult if not impossible for us to pray for ourselves. Beyond that fact, if sin is the root cause of our sickness, we may be blinded from even seeing it. In that case, it is good for us to be able to call on those who, like Mary, are in close fellowship with God, those who sit at His feet and know what to ask Him for.

When we are in sick or in need, God wants to give us a personal word. But as we study God's *written* Word and seek His *personal* word to us in our situations, we need to understand that He may not tell us everything we want to know in advance.

WHEN GOD DOESN'T TELL US EVERYTHING

The Lord's personal word to Mary and Martha was a message of great comfort and assurance. After all, this was Jesus talking. Mary and Martha both knew Him well and knew all about His teaching and His miracles. If anyone's words concerning their brother could be trusted, they were His.

But if we look at the timing of Jesus receiving word of Lazarus's illness, combined with the timing of His departure from Perea to Bethany (a good two-days' journey), it appears almost certain that Lazarus was already dead by the time the two sisters received His word. Not only that, it's entirely possible that Lazarus was dead by the time Jesus received word of the illness.

I can't help but wonder at the confusion Mary and Martha felt when they received Jesus' personal word that "this sickness is not unto death." Those words must have rung just a little bit hollow! I can just imagine them hearing that message, then looking at their brother's dead body and wondering if Jesus knew what He was talking about...or if He really cared about their predicament.

The fact is, while Mary and Martha had a personal word from Jesus, they did not have access to all the plans in His heart. No human being has that. The sisters couldn't know the particulars of how Jesus was going to work in their brother's situation. He didn't tell them that He knew about the death in advance. He didn't tell them that their brother's physical death would only be temporary. He didn't tell them He would arrive on the scene only after Lazarus's body had begun to decay in the tomb. And He didn't tell them His plan to personally raise their brother from the dead.

That's how hearing a personal word from God sometimes works, even today. As we pray for a word from God or for an outright healing or deliverance, we need to understand that there will be times when God's response leaves lots of blanks on the page. The understanding He gives us may be "part one" of ten parts...or a hundred parts. In other words, He may want us to receive enlightenment in a step-by-step or progressive way.

That's how God has always revealed Himself throughout history. The Bible wasn't written instantaneously, but progressively, starting with the basics of creation and the fall of humankind, moving through the process of redemption, and ending with the "end times" story found in the book of Revelation. We have the complete Bible available to us now, but it took more than fifteen centuries and forty-odd different writers to complete this one blessed Book.

God didn't reveal Himself all at once for the same reasons He so often doesn't reveal to us every aspect of how He handles our physical sicknesses or other difficulties.

First of all, God in His infinite wisdom knows that we wouldn't be able to handle knowing everything He had planned for us all at once. We might find ourselves tempted to move out ahead of Him—to accomplish by ourselves what He has planned to do for us.

Second, if He revealed everything to us up front, that would keep us from learning to trust Him and to have absolute faith that He is in control.

I believe that is partly why Jesus didn't fill in the blanks when it came to what He planned to do about Lazarus's sickness. Had He told Mary and Martha from the beginning that Lazarus would die, be buried, and then be raised from the dead, it is likely that they wouldn't have learned the lessons about faith that you'll read about as you continue on in this book.

Jesus wanted these two, dear, grieving women to learn to trust Him fully and completely. They already loved Him. He knew that. But they also needed to trust in His ability to control everything that happened to their little family.

When God gives us a personal word in our suffering, we don't *need* all the details up front. It's enough to know that the great Creator of the universe cares enough to speak to us *individually*.

BUT WHY JUST A WORD?

Jesus had sent Mary and Martha a personal word, and it was a personal word designed to expand and strengthen their faith and trust in Him. But that leaves us with some important questions: Why didn't Jesus just go to Bethany immediately and do for Mary and Martha what they had requested—and expected?

When Jesus finally arrived in Bethany, a bitterly disappointed and grieving Martha greeted Him at the outskirts of town and cried, "Lord, if You had been here, my brother would not have died" (John 11:21). In Martha's mind—and in the mind of her sister, who a short time later said the very same thing—it was too late for Jesus to do anything about her brother's sickness.

But within the realm of the heavenly Father's perfect plan, Jesus arrived right on time—not one moment too early, not one moment too late.

You see, there was more to be done in this story than a simple healing or resurrection. Jesus wanted to teach some people He loved very dearly what it meant to trust and obey Him, even in the worst of situations. And for Him to have come to Bethany before He did would have thwarted that plan.

We must remember that although Jesus loves each of us more deeply than we can fully comprehend and cares deeply when we are sick or hurting, everything He does and says is governed by a higher principle: doing what the Father calls Him to do when He calls Him to do it and in the manner He tells Him to do it.

Jesus was (and is) committed to the will of His Father, and that meant that His every decision was based on the Father's purposes and timetable for fulfilling that will. For example, He knew from the very beginning that His ultimate mission on earth was to give Himself over to the hands of those who wanted Him gone and to die a horrible death on the Cross. But He also knew that the Father had His own perfect timetable for that to happen. That is why the Gospels tell us repeatedly that although the Jewish religious authorities wanted to have Him killed—and appeared to have had chances to do just that—His time had not yet come. That event would only happen when the Father gave the green light.

When we or one of our loved ones is sick and hurting, we want God to move, and we want Him to move *right now*. It's quite natural to pray that way, and I don't think it's a bad thing to do so. But it's important that when we pray for God to move for us that we also pray like Job, who endured more than his share of suffering and who said, "Though He slay me, I will hope in Him" (Job 13:15). Jesus Himself, at His very moment of truth prayed, "Not what I will, but what You will" (Mark 14:36).

Jesus had told the anxious sisters that their brother's sickness would not end in death. While He didn't fill them in on the specifics of His plan, and didn't arrive right away like they wanted Him to, He let them know that He was in control and knew how the situation was going to end.

When we or a loved one is going through tough times of illness or other difficulties, we need to keep our eyes on two things: He knows what we're going through, and He knows how our situations will end...for our good and for His glory.

This Lazarus situation wasn't over—not by a long shot. Jesus had promised Mary and Martha that their brother's sickness would not end in death, and it was a promise He was on His way to keeping in a spectacular, miraculous way.

--- 2 ---

God, Do You Really Care...

WHEN I'M AFRAID?

O ne of the current hit television series at this writing is
a sometimes-gruesome little "reality program" called
Fear Factor.

In each weekly episode, six contestants attempt to face down
some of their most primal fears in order to claim a cash prize of
$50,000. The show features people doing some of the most bizarre
things ever seen on television, including putting themselves in what
appear to be life-threatening situations and eating live insects (and
other gross creatures). Every stunt they pull and every "meal" they
eat is designed to challenge the participants to overcome their deep-
est fears in order to win the big bucks.

Faced with what are in reality "manufactured fears," the contestants are never in any real danger of losing life or limb. Instead, they are faced with situations that cause them to *feel* fear.

In real life, however, we don't have to deal with manufactured fears. Who needs an imitation when you've got the genuine article! In the course of our lives, we're faced with all kinds of things that stir fear in our hearts. Fear really is a factor in our lives, even for those of us who trust Jesus Christ for our salvation.

Why is that?

Simply because we're human, and though we're heaven-bound children of God, we're still subject to human responses and emotions. For that reason, we can suffer many fears—fears that affect us, infect us, and sometimes control us.

Even the disciples of Jesus Christ, men who walked for three-plus years at the side of God's Son, experienced fear. One of those incidents took place at the time of Lazarus's illness and death.

WE'RE GOING *WHERE?*

Before I move on in the story, I want to pose some questions. Would you board a commercial flight if you knew there was a good chance that one of its passengers was a terrorist bent on bringing the plane down in midflight? Would you walk through some of the more hostile areas of Iraq or Afghanistan with an American flag on your back? Would you eat something if you knew there was a fifty-fifty chance it could cause you to become deathly ill?

Only if you had a death wish!

There are some things plain old common sense keeps us from doing, because we know better than to intentionally or carelessly put ourselves in harm's way.

That's exactly how the twelve disciples saw what Jesus was asking them to do when He said, "Let us go to Judea again" (John 11:7).

Judea was the Roman region of Palestine (now Israel) that included the holy city of Jerusalem as well as the little village of Bethany, where Jesus' close friends Lazarus, Mary, and Martha lived. It was also the hub of Jewish religious life in those days. And at that particular time, it was a hotbed of hostility toward Jesus from the religious leadership—those who wanted more than anything to put an end to Him and the "movement" He appeared to be starting.

John records three previous scenes of potential violence against Jesus in Judea.

In John 5, the apostle tells us that the Jewish leadership wanted to kill Him because He was (at least in their eyes) breaking the Sabbath. But that was only half of it. He had also called God His Father, which in the Jewish faith essentially meant claiming equality with God.

In chapter 8, John tells us that the Jews had actually picked up stones to kill Him because He had made this stunning claim: "Truly,

truly I say to you, before Abraham was born, I am" (John 8:58). The Jews immediately recognized "I Am" as the name God had used from ancient days to identify Himself as the one and only eternal God. To their ears, that sounded like blasphemy, and deserving of death.

Later, Jesus was again threatened with stoning during the Feast of Dedication in Jerusalem. And once again, it was because of claims He made that the Jews considered blasphemous. A group of Jews had asked Jesus to plainly tell them whether or not He was the Messiah. After pointing out that He had already told them who He really was, Jesus shocked them by saying, "I and the Father are one" (John 10:30).

Now, with the desire to kill Him still burning white hot, Jesus told His men that they were going to jump right back into the frying pan. The disciples, however, were in no mood to even think about heading back to Judea, a place they knew wasn't safe. They asked Him, "Rabbi, the Jews were just now seeking to stone You, and are You going there again?" (John 11:8).

WHAT'S ALL THIS "US" TALK?

It's easy to read dialogue in familiar Bible passages and totally miss the "tone of voice." And I can just hear the disciples asking that last question in the same tone of voice we might reserve for someone about to do something reckless and foolish: *"Are you out of your mind?"*

At a glance, the disciples seemed concerned about Jesus' safety. But what they were really doing was camouflaging their own fear under concern for Jesus. When they asked Him, "Are You going back there again?" what they *really* meant was, "Are You taking *us* back there again?"

The disciples were afraid to go back to Judea. There were people there—people in positions of power and authority—who wanted Jesus dead. And if they wanted Jesus dead, His closest followers had to believe they wanted *them* dead, too.

If they'd had a better grasp on who their Master really was, maybe they wouldn't have been quite so afraid to walk back into the danger zone with Him. But these men had a lot of growing to do— just as you and I do—and the thought of heading back into that hostile environment obviously terrified them.

Jesus, however, showed no fear at all.

He knew He had a great God-ordained appointment to glorify the Father and Himself and to make an impact for the kingdom, and He was intent on obeying God's call no matter what.

Jesus' obvious courage in the face of such a clear and deadly threat was a nonverbal lesson for the disciples about the importance of focus. You see, Jesus wasn't focused on the indisputable fact that the Jewish leadership in Judea wanted to kill Him. In fact, He had a focus that overshadowed everything else: He was committed to continuing His life of perfect obedience to the Father, no matter what kind of worldly danger it presented. That's because He was completely and perfectly "in tune" with the Father, and knew that nothing in the universe could harm Him until the appointed time.

It was a lesson the disciples had been taught, but apparently hadn't yet *caught*.

FEAR 101

The Gospels record another incident in which Jesus made a "let us go" statement. The fourth chapter of Mark records how after a day of preaching and teaching on the shores of the Sea of Galilee, Jesus said to the disciples, "*Let us go* over to the other side" (Mark 4:35).

Fear may have been the farthest emotion from their minds when the disciples set out on their voyage across the sea. Their boat, as well as several others that followed, sliced its way through the serene blue waters and all was well. Acquainted as they were with this body of water, the Lord's men were as calm as they would have been relaxing at the home of a friend—maybe more so.

But everything changed in what seemed like the space of a few heartbeats. Suddenly, their very lives were in jeopardy.

The Sea of Galilee is known to this day for sudden and violent windstorms, and as the disciples' boat made its way across the lake, a violent, powerful storm smacked into their boat like a giant fist.

Huge waves suddenly rose up all around them, threatening to swamp the boat. The disciples were more than frightened—they were in absolute panic. At least four of them were fishermen and had, no doubt, lived through more than their share of Sea of Galilee windstorms. But as the wind-whipped waves crashed over the side of the boat, they screamed out in terror to Jesus, "Teacher, do You not care that we are perishing?" (Mark 4:38).

Now, of course the disciples had to know that Jesus cared. At the very least, they knew He had no interest in drowning with them in the middle of the Sea of Galilee. So why did they ask such a question? Because Jesus was in the rear of the boat...fast asleep. And not only asleep, He was asleep on a cushion. That tells me that Jesus hadn't just "nodded off" but that He had gone to the back of the boat fully intending to take a nap as they made their passage.

Though Jesus awoke to the sound of the wind, waves, and screaming disciples, He remained perfectly calm. Rather than scrambling around in the boat and helping the disciples bail water, Jesus rose to His feet, quickly surveyed the situation, then uttered what I consider one of the most amazing statements in the New Testament: "Peace, be still" (Mark 4:39, KJV).

Wouldn't it have made more sense for Him to say, "*Storm*, be still!"? After all, it was the windstorm that had caused all the panic. But Jesus wasn't just speaking to the storm. He was also speaking to the men in the boat. Yes, they were in the midst of the gale, but they were also in the midst of God's will. When they had set out to cross the sea, they had done so in obedience to the Lord's clear command.

And what they had not yet learned was that the will of God will never take you where the grace of God can't keep you.

With the storm settled—the waves and the disciples' hammering hearts returning to normal—Jesus took the opportunity to confront His men about their panic attack. Just moments before, they had screamed at Him, basically accusing Him of not caring that they were about to die. I can just imagine him looking from man to man, face to face, and then saying, "Why are you so timid?" (Mark 4:40).

I don't know about you, but if I were in a little fishing boat that only moments before was about to be swallowed up by the sea, I'd probably be more than a little stunned that someone would ask such a question. *Why are we so timid?* The disciples must have given each other sidelong glances. *Timid? Didn't You see what was happening to us? Didn't You see that black sky and feel that lashing wind? Didn't you notice the size of those monster waves? And You ask why we're so timid?*

But class was in session at that moment, and Jesus had an important lesson for His men. He wanted them to understand that when they were walking—or in this case, sailing—with Him, they didn't need to be afraid of anything, even of those things that their rational human minds told them they *should* fear. And why? Because when they were with Him and trusting and obeying Him, nothing would happen to them that He didn't allow.

Jesus was comfortable and fearless in a really bad situation because He knew what God had sent Him to earth to do, and knew that nothing would happen to Him that the Father didn't ordain and approve.

This scene tells me a few things about our walk with Jesus. First, it tells me that we can be perfectly obedient and in the will of God and still have to endure the storms of life—and the fears that accompany them. More importantly, it tells me that even in the midst of the most terrifying life storms, we can be in a place of peace…and that place is in the will of God.

But it also tells me that those sorts of scary, fearful situations could be a God-sent test. Yes, the situation itself may be real, imminent, and dangerous, but it very well could be a test to see if we are walking in fear or in complete trust in a God who has proved Himself trustworthy times beyond counting.

MEANWHILE, BACK IN PEREA...

Jesus had a specific plan and reason for going to Judea: to see His friends Mary and Martha and to perform an amazing miracle for them, a shocking reversal of the laws of nature, which would glorify both the Father and the Son.

But when Jesus first told the disciples that they would be going with Him back to Judea, He didn't say anything about Lazarus or

Bethany. At that point in the story, the disciples had no idea why Jesus would want to go to a place where there were people lying in wait for Him.

A frightened group of men had a very simple and direct question for Jesus: "Are you really going to Judea?" It was a logical, reasonable question. But Jesus' answer no doubt had them scratching their heads—and probably feeling a bit frustrated: "Are there not twelve hours of daylight? A man who walks by day will not stumble, for he sees by this world's light. It is when he walks by night that he stumbles, for he has no light" (John 11:9–10, NIV).

Now if I had been one of the disciples, I might have asked Jesus what all that talk of light and darkness had to do with the price of camels in Egypt. After all, what I really wanted to know was, "Are You really intending to take us back to a place where we know there are people gunning for You—and probably us, too? Can't You answer with a simple yes or no? And while You're at it, why don't You tell us why in the world we would want to go back there, anyway."

A DEEPER LESSON

Quite often during His earthly ministry, Jesus answered very direct questions with what appeared to be elusive or evasive answers. Sometimes it seemed like His answers had nothing at all to do with what was asked. But when He did that, He invariably had a deeper spiritual lesson in His answer than what His questioners might have had in mind. He would sometimes be answering the bigger, nonverbal questions *behind* the question.

Instead of talking to them about the merits of strolling back into the killing zone, He began to speak about what time of day they would be traveling: when there was daylight.

At this time in history, the Romans had constructed an amazing system of highways and roads throughout the empire, which made travel much easier. But what they couldn't do in that day and age was light those roads for nighttime travel. Because of that, nighttime travel was possible only when there was sufficient moonlight to light the traveler's way.

Obviously, however, Jesus had something more profound in mind than Roman Empire travel tips. He spoke figuratively, using the illuminating light of the sun as an analogy to teach them to put fear in its place.

In the Bible, words such as *day* and *light* refer to God's righteousness—that which is of the Word of God and in the will of God. On the other hand, the words *night* and *darkness* point us toward evil and unrighteousness.

Jesus, then, was seeking to teach His men the spiritual principle of walking in and being governed by the illumination of the light of God. When they did that, He was saying, they didn't need to allow their fears to paralyze them or keep them from courageous obedience.

We see that in the Gospel of John, in which the apostle proclaims Jesus using variations of the word *light*. John begins his Gospel by using the analogy of light to refer to Jesus' life and works on earth (1:4–9). Later, John twice quotes Jesus as calling Himself "the Light of the World" (8:12, 9:5).

John continues that theme of darkness and light in his first epistle:

> This is the message we have heard from Him and announce to you, that God is Light, and in Him there is no darkness at all. If we say that we have fellowship with Him and yet walk in the darkness, we lie and do not practice the truth; but if we walk in the Light as He Himself is in the Light, we have fellowship with one another, and the blood of Jesus His Son cleanses us from all sin.
>
> I JOHN 1:5–7

Now, you don't need a master's degree in literature to know that when an author repeats something the way John repeated this "darkness and light" motif, then you'd better pay attention, because there's a bigger message than what first meets the eye.

The bottom line? Jesus Himself was the "daylight" in which His followers must walk. If they were walking with Him, walking in His will, walking in His illumination, walking in His protection, they had nothing to fear from dark or threatening circumstances.

When Jesus recognized that the disciples were frightened at the prospect of heading into Judea, He didn't tell them that they would just wait until things cooled down there, then head out. That would have thwarted the divine appointment He had with Lazarus and his sisters. And He didn't allow them to give in to their fears and take a safer course. Instead, He told them that they would walk toward Judea, and would do it during that time when the sun illuminated the road.

On such a path, flooded with the light of His presence, they would gain the right perspective on the things that caused them to fear.

CHOOSING TO WALK IN THE LIGHT

All of us will face things in life that frighten us, but we are only defeated by our fears when we allow them to keep us from staying on the course God has given us to run. God wants us to live a life of fulfillment and joy in Him, but if there is one thing that will keep us from doing just that, it's fear. Fear holds us back, cripples us, blinds us, and keeps us from hearing from God or obeying when He speaks. I've seen too many examples of fear keeping people from enjoying fulfilling human relationships, from taking significant steps in their career, and, worst of all, from being used effectively for the kingdom of God.

Too many of us avoid or run from the prospects that frighten us. Fearing rejection, we avoid close contact with other people. Fearing failure, we simply stop trying to accomplish anything, be it in our professional lives or in any potential ministry God has for us. And fearing people, we keep our mouths shut when we should be talking to friends, coworkers, and neighbors about all that God has done for us.

When we run from the things that frighten us, we've handed Satan the victory in a gift-wrapped box with a bow on top. We've essentially waved the white flag and said to the devil, "You win!" Our paralysis in the face of fear gives victory to an enemy who loves nothing more than to freeze us in our tracks, to cripple us, and to render us useless for God's kingdom.

Can there be any better definition of walking in darkness?

FACING YOUR FEARS

I once heard the story of a man experiencing some pretty intense pain in his belly, along with some other potentially serious symptoms. But he refused to go see his doctor, only because he was afraid of what the diagnosis might be.

Finally, after several sleepless nights and the not-so-gentle prodding of his loving and concerned wife, this fearful man went to the doctor. The diagnosis? Acute appendicitis, a common and easily treatable condition when exposed early—but a potentially fatal one when it's not diagnosed and treated.

Refusing to go to a doctor because we're afraid of what he might tell us would be the very definition of foolishness, wouldn't it? But it's just as foolish for us to avoid confronting the things that make us fearful. Simply dodging or closing our eyes to life's issues won't make them go away. Death will always be death, sickness will always be sickness, and failure will always be failure. And when we refuse to confront our fears over those things, we choose to walk in darkness and to avoid reality.

When we are fearful, no matter what may be causing our fear, it's important for us to be honest with ourselves and with God about what's really scaring us. Trying to appear strong and fearless on the outside while we're in complete turmoil on the inside gets us nowhere.

Psalm 34 is probably my favorite Bible passage on dealing honestly with fear. In this psalm, David tells us how he handled the multitude of fears that confronted him during the many colorful chapters of his walk with the Lord: "I sought the LORD, and He answered me, and delivered me from all my fears" (Psalm 34:4).

David didn't deny being afraid. He didn't slap a happy face over that which truly frightened him, or live in denial, insisting that "everything is just fine" when it really wasn't. Instead of denying the fear in his life, he did something with it. He took it to the one place where we can all receive comfort when we're afraid: to God Himself!

Don't run from or deny your fears. That's dishonest, and only makes things worse.

Don't run from your fears. You *will* have to face them one day, and you can never grow in your faith until you do.

God cares when we are afraid, and He has given us a way to confront and defeat our fears. It's by exposing them to the light He gives us through His Son, Jesus Christ.

FEAR'S STRONG ANTIDOTE

More than 360 times in the Bible we read variations of God telling us not to be afraid. And time after time we see Jesus personally demonstrating what it takes to live lives under God's control and not under the control of fear.

One of the many things Jesus came to deliver us from was fear, but far too many believers still allow their fears—real, rational fears as well as fears they've cooked up in their own minds—to control them. But why are so many believers absolutely crippled by these anxieties? I believe it's because too many of us are dealing with them from positions of darkness, and not from the position of walking in the light of Jesus Christ.

This is what Jesus was talking about when He said, "If anyone walks in the night, he stumbles, because the light is not in him" (John 11:10).

If you've ever lost power in your home on a dark, moonless night, you know how frustrating—and sometimes dangerous—it can be to try to grope your way through the house. What had once been familiar and comfortable becomes an unseen maze of obstacles, some of which can cause stubbed toes, bruised shins, and worse.

That illustrates what Jesus was saying to the disciples. When we as believers walk in the darkness of fear rather than in the light of Jesus Christ, whatever we try to accomplish and wherever we try to go will be thwarted. We will trip, stumble, and fall on our faces.

Hard as it may be to feel your way from one dark room to another without running into something or hurting yourself, it's just as difficult to work your way through a season of fear without using the right standards—the ones God has given us in His Word. Self-talk and gritting your teeth really aren't much help in the grip of paralyzing fear and constant worry. Even counseling, worthy as that might be at times, won't help you when you face life-crippling fears sent by the enemy of your soul.

The only thing that will ultimately defeat your fears once and for all is your focus on and application of the truth of God's Word in your daily life. For example, the Bible tells us that if you want to overcome the fear of man, you should make Jesus Christ your Lord and confess Him openly before men:

But even if you should suffer for the sake of righteousness, you are blessed. *And do not fear their intimidation, and do not be troubled,* but sanctify Christ as Lord in your hearts, always being ready to make a defense to everyone who asks you to give an account for the hope that is in you, yet with gentleness and reverence.

1 PETER 3:14–15

The devil wants to hold you hostage to the fear of people, but God wants you to be fearless in proclaiming Jesus Christ as your Lord and Savior. When you do that, you are making the highest proclamation that can be made. Once you make it, you'll know that other people no longer have the last say when it comes to you talking about your faith.

The Bible also sets the standard for worry, which I would define as fear over what may or may not happen to us next. It's that feeling of insecurity over the future, over how we're going to care for ourselves and our families.

If we think about it long enough, we'll find plenty to worry about. We can worry about our finances, our families, our health—just to name a few such items. But Jesus spoke clearly to this fear as well: "But seek first His [God's] kingdom and His righteousness, and all these things will be added to you" (Matthew 6:33).

When Jesus told His followers to seek God and His righteousness first, He was telling them to walk in the light of God, the place where fear, worry, and insecurity are exposed for what they are. What was Jesus talking about when He said that "all these things shall be added to you"? He was speaking about the basics we need for life, the very things over which so many of us fret and worry.

> "Therefore I tell you, do not worry about your life, what you will eat or drink; or about your body, what you will wear. Is not life more important than food, and the body more important than clothes? Look at the birds of the air; they do not sow or reap or store away in barns, and yet your heavenly Father feeds them. Are you not much more valuable than they?"
>
> MATTHEW 6:25–26, NIV

Have you ever heard about a sparrow on Prozac? I don't know about you, but I've never heard about a bird with an ulcer or high blood pressure. That's because these creatures simply go about their business of gathering up food for themselves and their young. Birds don't stress and fret about the future, because God has built into them the instinctive knowledge that He cares for them and meets their needs. He will provide their daily worm, or whatever else they need to live and thrive.

THE GREATEST FEAR

While there are many things we might fear, most people will tell you that they fear death more than anything else. In some respects, the fear of death is natural and healthy; it's the "self-preservation" instinct God has given us so that we don't take our lives lightly, and unnecessarily put ourselves in danger.

While the Bible doesn't downplay or deny the pain we feel when a loved one dies or when we face death ourselves, it does tell us that death is not the end of those who believe in Jesus Christ. Our Lord personally defeated death once and for all through His death on the Cross and His resurrection three days later.

As children of Adam and Eve, members of a fallen race, each of us must face that final enemy one day, no matter how consistently we work out, eat right, and shun harmful habits. As someone once said, "The one thing we know for certain about life is this: No one gets out of it alive!"

But even there, even in that "valley of the shadow" which all of us must enter one day, we walk in the radiant, encircling, enveloping light of the Lord Jesus Christ. *And where He leads us, He will keep us.* We can walk in the daylight of His comforting presence right up until that moment when we step into eternal daylight—and see Him face to face.

Jesus understood that His men were afraid of the deadly dangers they faced in Judea. And He cared, taking the time to teach them some principles on how to face and defeat their fears.

He does the same for us today as He allows us—even *encourages* us—to take our fears to Him. Shining the light of His infinite goodness and grace on every dark corner of our lives, He helps us put those fears in their place.

Behind us.

3

God, Do You Really Care...
WHEN I'M CONFUSED?

Confusion is as common to humanity as hiccups or complaining about the weather.

And the people who say they're never confused? Well, those are the ones who are *really* confused! They don't even know how little they know.

It's no different for Christ's followers.

I don't think I've ever met a believer who hasn't at some point in life been confused about what God was doing in his or her life. Sometimes we're perplexed or thrown off balance by the way God answers our prayers—or makes us wait for answers. It's even more confusing when He gives us a personal word confirmed by the written Word telling us one thing...while it seems for all the world like

He's taking us in another direction altogether.

Do you ever find God confusing? Welcome to the club! You're in company with some of the true giants of faith. From one end of the Bible to the other, we read of God confusing people—including His most loyal, loving servants. Time and again, we see the Almighty doing things that defy human logic—or even what seems like good common sense.

In the Bible we see God

- planting a very appealing tree in the middle of the Garden of Eden...*then telling Adam and Eve not to eat from it;*
- keeping His promise to Abraham by giving him a miracle son...*then asking him to sacrifice his boy on an altar;*
- leading His people out of Egypt to the very edge of the Red Sea...*just as the army of Pharaoh closed in on them;*
- allowing Israel to face an imminent and overwhelming enemy invasion...*then sending a choir out to march in front of the army.*

It doesn't stop with the Old Testament. In fact, Jesus Himself often did and said things that completely flummoxed His closest followers.

"L O R D ... I   D O N ' T   U N D E R S T A N D"

In the story of Lazarus, we read how Jesus confused two of His dearest friends—in a time of great stress and sorrow. First of all, when Mary and Martha summoned Him to Bethany to heal Lazarus, He didn't come for two more days. Instead, He sent a message that their brother's illness wouldn't end in death. What He had seemed to promise, however, didn't happen! Lazarus died anyway.

In the last chapter, I talked about how when the time was right—Jesus' time and not Mary and Martha's—He frightened the disciples by announcing that they would be heading to Judea. And then he dealt with their understandable fears in a way that didn't make sense to them at all.

But that wasn't the end of the confusion.

After Jesus had addressed the disciples' fears, He told them why they were going to Judea: to do a miracle on behalf of Lazarus. But what was so perplexing about that announcement was the way He worded it: "Our friend Lazarus has fallen asleep; but I go, so that I may awaken him out of sleep" (John 11:11).

Asleep? The disciples were a plain-talking bunch, and they took Jesus to mean that Lazarus was literally asleep. And if he was just sleeping, they reasoned, he must be getting better. But by now you know that when Jesus said that Lazarus had fallen asleep, what He meant was that he had died of his illness. And then He "clarified" that fact by saying something even more confusing! "Lazarus is dead, and I am glad for your sakes that I was not there, so that you may believe; but let us go to him" (John 11:14–15).

He was—*what?* Glad that He hadn't been there? Glad that Lazarus had missed a healing touch and died? And now he was dead, but they were about to risk their lives to go see him? This wasn't adding up at all! What was the Master talking about?

Did Jesus care that He had confused the disciples?

At first, it appears that He was just playing word games with them—"playing with their heads," as the phrase goes. Wouldn't it have been simpler—not to mention time saving—for Jesus to have simply said, "Our friend Lazarus has died, and we're going to Bethany so I can raise him from the dead"? And wouldn't it have been easier on Mary and Martha to have simply told them, "Your brother Lazarus will die from this illness, but that won't be the end of his story! I'll come by in a few days and raise him from the dead!"

He could have declared those things.

He could have made it easier to understand.

But He didn't.

Why not? Why didn't He?

Jesus could just as easily have spoken plainly to the disciples about Lazarus's death and His plans to raise him. But something He said in this passage—something confusing on its very face—tells us that He had a special objective in mind for the disciples that day. "I am glad for your sakes that I was not there," He told them, "*so that you may believe.*"

I know if I had been on the scene with Jesus and the disciples at that moment, I would have been rocked back on my heels by those words. Up to that point, the disciples had seen Jesus do astounding miracles of healing—including curing someone from a distance and even raising the dead. And now He was saying He was glad that Lazarus hadn't been healed?

How confusing can you get!

Jesus, however, had a plan. He always has a plan! And in this case, it was a plan to do far more than the miracle of raising His friend Lazarus from the dead. He was about to teach the disciples lessons of faith they would remember to their dying day.

God cares when we are confused, but there are times when He must intentionally allow that to happen—in order to accomplish a higher purpose in our lives.

He wants to change our thinking.

And for many of us, that's a pretty tall order.

A CHANGE IN OUR THINKING

Have you ever seen one of those lab experiments where animal behavioralists put some poor mouse in a maze to see how long it takes him to reach the food at its center? You feel just a little bit sorry for the hungry rodent as he scampers his way into dead end after dead end. Eventually—if the mouse is intelligent and persistent enough—he reaches his ultimate goal: lunch!

For many of us, life can seem like a maze. I think you know what I mean. One moment we think we're headed in the right direction, only to find that the path we've chosen smacks into a dead end. We change direction over and over, only to find more dead ends. It can be frustrating, but there is one thing we can be sure of: Our God cares when we feel lost, directionless, and confused.

Remember when Jesus looked out over all those people milling around, the crowds who had come to see Him? Scripture says, "When he saw the crowds, he had compassion on them, because they were harassed and helpless, like sheep without a shepherd" (Matthew 9:36, NIV).

Why, then, doesn't He do something about our bewilderment? Why doesn't God just reach down and guide us through the mazes of our lives? Why does He sometimes allow us to go through the confusion—confusion over our own lives and confusion over what He's saying? I believe it's because God understands us inside out, and knows very well what it takes to teach us deeper spiritual truths. Sometimes understanding—those breakthrough "ah-hah!" moments—only comes through struggle.

Most of us probably remember being a school kid struggling with math problems. We probably also remember that when we asked Miss Whitworth for help, she wouldn't come right out and hand us the answers. Instead, she gave us little clues and tidbits so that we could figure things out for ourselves. That's because any good teacher knows that simply giving children the answers to problems they struggle over won't help them learn the principles *behind* the problems. Sure, they may pencil in "the right answer," but they'll have no idea how they got there—and won't be able to solve another problem just like it.

So it is with God. He will sometimes give us what seem like confusing directions instead of a simple 1-2-3 answer because He wants to move our thinking from the physical realm to the spiritual.

That's what Jesus was doing when He told the disciples that Lazarus was asleep.

WHY "SLEEP"?

Jesus spoke mysteriously—even confusingly—about Lazarus's passing because He wanted to change the disciples' thinking on the subject of death itself.

Jesus knew that His little band of men hadn't yet come to a point in their walk with Him where they were able to comprehend major life issues—including death—with spiritual eyes and ears. They had seen the most incredible miracles ever performed and listened to some of the most profound teaching ever taught. Even so, they were still living, walking, and thinking in the natural.

Jesus wanted to "bait" the disciples into thinking differently about death, so He used a new and different language concerning the subject. He didn't fear death, and He wanted the disciples—and us—to understand that for the believer, death is not to be feared, but looked at as a homecoming, a graduation into something far greater than this earthly life.

The New Testament often speaks metaphorically of death using variations of the word *sleep*. (For examples, see 1 Corinthians 11:30, 15:51; 1 Thessalonians 4:14). That is fitting, because we know that sleep doesn't end our existence or change who we are. It simply puts us in a different realm of consciousness. In the same way, we don't cease to be just because our bodies die. Far from it! In fact, we're more alive than ever. We've just moved on into an eternal realm, in the presence of the Lord. As the apostle Paul put it, "We are of good courage...and prefer rather to be absent from the body and to be at home with the Lord" (2 Corinthians 5:8).

It was also a comforting and assuring picture of physical death, because none of us fears sleep. Most of us crave more of it! Sleep is harmless, beneficial, and even necessary if we want to be physically healthy. It's even a pleasant feeling to lie down after a long day, relax, and let sleep gently carry us away.

God wants to move us from thinking on the purely physical or temporal level to a spiritual and eternal level, and sometimes He moves us in that direction by saying and doing things that confuse us. He does that to change our thinking, to nudge us from our limited perspective to His infinite perspective. And as He does, He is also working to develop and strengthen our faith.

"SHOW-ME" CHRISTIANS?

Most of us know that Missouri is commonly called the "Show-Me State," a nickname widely attributed to a turn-of-the-century congressman named Willard Duncan Vandiver. In a speech in Philadelphia, Congressman Vandiver declared that he wasn't impressed by "frothy eloquence," adding, "I am from Missouri. You have to show me."

While the "show me" attitude might be a good one for politics, it's absolutely backward when it comes to a life of faith. Sadly, too many Christians demonstrate a "show me" way of thinking when it comes to their relationship with God. By that, I mean they don't trust God to keep the promises He's already made in His written Word. Instead, they need to actually "see something" before they will believe.

The writer of the letter to the Hebrews tells us, "Now faith is the assurance of things hoped for, the conviction of things not seen" (11:1). In other words, faith is believing God and taking Him completely at His word *before* we've had the opportunity to see Him move on our behalf.

That can be frustrating and confusing to many believers, but we need to understand that God has so constructed this life of faith that we will only see after we believe. For that reason, if we choose to believe Him and trust in Him simply because He is a God who keeps His word, then there is no limit to where our walk of faith can take us.

Time after time in the Bible we see examples of people believing God, acting on what they knew He wanted from them, then receiving a promised blessing. For example, Abraham believed God and left his life of security and wealth to pursue God's leading. Turning his back on all he had ever known, Abraham committed to going where God wanted him to go and doing what God wanted him to do.

From virtually cover to cover, the Bible brims over with passages on the importance of faith. We are saved through faith (Ephesians 2:8–9), but we are also told that we must live by faith: "For in it the righteousness of God is revealed from faith to faith; as it is written, 'But the righteous man shall live by faith'" (Romans 1:17).

But what is the evidence that we're living by faith? It's simply this: We live, act, and speak as though God is telling the truth even when we don't have any empirical evidence. In other words, we're obedient to Him and trust in Him even when what He's saying and doing in our lives confuses us.

CONFUSION AND COMMITMENT

When Jesus gave the disciples their marching orders by saying, "Let us go to him," one of the disciples made a rather stunning statement. John records it this way: "Therefore Thomas, who is called

Didymus, said to his fellow disciples, 'Let us also go, so that we may die with Him'" (John 11:16).

Thomas? Most of us remember Thomas for his doubt, his hesitation. Remember? Thomas was the last of the disciples to see Jesus after His resurrection. He went on record that he just wouldn't believe Jesus had risen from the dead unless he could actually touch the wounds Jesus received at the Crucifixion (see John 20:24–29).

While most believers remember Thomas as the doubter, few remember him as the one who spoke with such boldness when Jesus called the disciples to follow Him to Judea. As with the others, Thomas wasn't focused on miracles as much as on the danger he knew awaited them. But that wasn't what was most important to Thomas that day. In his mind, it was better to go with Jesus and face death with Him, rather than stay safe where he was—without Him.

The disciples had reached a crossroads in their walk with Jesus. If they followed Him, they would get to see the miracle of life—the raising of Lazarus—but that meant being willing to risk dying with Him by walking into a highly dangerous place.

As a group, Jesus' disciples weren't the most educated or gifted people He could have chosen. But they weren't stupid, either. They knew that what Jesus was asking them to do was, at least by all human reasoning, foolish. But when Jesus called them to follow Him back to Bethany, He was not only giving them an opportunity to see a miracle, He was also testing their commitment.

Sometimes, when it seems that what God is calling us to do is confusing, it's because He's testing our commitment to Him to see if we're willing to lay aside our own desires and choose the way of obedience to Him.

Even when His way makes no earthly sense.

Even when following Him could mean death.

DYING IN ORDER TO LIVE

Jesus taught the principle many times in many different ways: *You have to die in order to truly live the life I have for you.*

Not long after Jesus raised Lazarus from the dead, He said it this way to Philip and Andrew, two of His disciples:

> "I tell you the truth, unless a kernel of wheat falls to the ground and dies, it remains only a single seed. But if it dies, it produces many seeds. The man who loves his life will lose it, while the man who hates his life in this world will keep it for eternal life. Whoever serves me must follow me; and where I am, my servant also will be. My Father will honor the one who serves me."
>
> JOHN 12:24–26, NIV

Again, this can be a confusing statement when we don't fully understand that Jesus was speaking figuratively. At first glance, the phrase "a man who hates his life in this world" makes us scratch our heads. Was He saying our lives here on earth are worthless? Was He saying that all we have to live for is dying so we can get to heaven?

No, He was aiming at a deeper spiritual application here. It's tied up in the analogy of how wheat plants sprout, grow, and produce edible grain. Jesus pointed out that wheat can only reproduce when grains of wheat fall from the stalk to the ground and "die"—at least in regard to what they were before. When that happens, that one kernel produces countless other kernels.

But how does this apply to us? What does it mean for us to die in this context? It really isn't rocket science. It simply means saying no to what we want, and yes to everything God wants of us. It means being wholeheartedly committed to doing the will of God, even when it involves denying our own desires. It means heeding and obeying what Jesus taught when He told the disciples, "If anyone wishes to come after Me, he must deny himself, and take up his cross and follow Me. For whoever wishes to save his life will lose it; but whoever loses his life for My sake will find it" (Matthew 16:24–25).

Outside of our receiving salvation through Jesus Christ, there is no greater decision a Christian can make than the one to "die to self." It's not only a big decision, it's a terribly difficult one to follow through with, simply because of our selfish human nature.

It reminds me of the old saying, "Everybody wants to go to heaven, but nobody wants to die." Of course, with the exception of those of us who are around when Jesus returns for His church, no one will see the kingdom of heaven without first dying physically. But when Jesus thoroughly confused the disciples by leading them into a situation that presented a very real threat of death, He was using that threat to make an even more important spiritual point: They had to be willing to die an inner spiritual death in order to follow Him.

This is one of the many paradoxes of true faith in Jesus Christ, and it can be confusing to many who are either nonbelievers or new to the faith. But Jesus was teaching the disciples a lesson all of us need to hear and heed for ourselves. And it is this: "Once you die, then you can begin living."

I know in my own life that my self wants what my self wants. But I also know that it is only when I daily decide to put aside my own wants and make Jesus my only desire that—in that moment—He shows me more of Himself. Only then do I begin to see spiritual fruit in my life.

Jesus' challenge to the disciples—and to us—is simple but life-changing. Were they willing to risk everything, including their physical lives, for Him? Were they willing to die to themselves and say yes to what God wanted no matter what the cost? Were they willing to follow Him to a place they knew to be dangerous, even though it made no earthly sense?

That, brothers and sisters, is Jesus' world, and He came so that we could be a part of it. It's a world where He willingly and joyfully submitted Himself to the will of His Father in heaven so that He could accomplish something far greater than His own comfort and safety.

Salvation for you, me, and all who would put their faith in Him.

HOW CAN WE KNOW?

Dying to self is a confusing proposition.

Your spirit says yes, your mind says no. Your spirit says, "Go for it," your body says, "No way!" The Spirit of God within you says, "Do it now," your own will and desires rebel and kick up a fuss.

Let's just come right out and admit it...it's confusing! How do we even know when and if we've accomplished it? How can we be certain we've done what Jesus has asked us to do? Here's what I think it boils down to: *Have you chosen to be content in the situations God has placed you in, no matter how confusing they may be?*

The apostle Paul is probably the second-best biblical example—outside of Jesus—of a man who had died to self. In his letter to the Philippian church, he wrote, "Not that I speak from want, for *I have learned to be content in whatever circumstances I am*" (Philippians 4:11).

If you, like the apostle Paul, have chosen to be content in every situation God has placed you in, no matter how perplexing or confusing, then you truly have died to self. But if you are one who complains—to yourself, to others, and to God—then you've not yet died to self.

God takes a serious view of complaining. Nowhere is that more evident than in the story of Israel's Exodus from Egypt. The Lord had given them a joyous promise of their very own homeland in Canaan—but He also warned them that they were going to have to trust Him as they made their way out of Egypt.

It wasn't going to be a Sunday stroll in the park. The Israelites would have to explicitly trust God for the very basics of life such as food and water. They would have to trust their ability to protect them from enemies. But God had already promised them, "I have come down to deliver them from the power of the Egyptians, and to bring them up from that land to a good and spacious land, to a land flowing with milk and honey, to the place of the Canaanite and the Hittite and the Amorite and the Perizzite and the Hivite and the Jebusite" (Exodus 3:8).

Incredibly, however, no sooner had the people left the bondage of Egypt than they started looking over their shoulders and longing for the security they believed they'd left behind them—the "security" of slavery to a cruel and evil tyrant. They complained because they needed water, complained because they wanted meat to eat instead of manna from heaven, complained because they were afraid of the enemies who came against them.

Because we know how the story ended up, it's easy for us to wonder what was really at the heart of those complaints. The Lord had given the people of Israel His word, but He also backed up that word by performing incredible miracles they had heard and seen for themselves. They had witnessed firsthand how God sent plagues on Egypt because a stubborn Pharaoh refused to obey the voice of God and set His people free. They had seen how He parted the Red Sea so that they could escape Pharaoh's army.

They had seen the nourishing, delicious "bread of heaven" form on the ground every morning like dew.

Yet all they could do was gripe, moan, and whine.

And why? Because although they had left Egypt physically, they had never left Egypt *in their hearts*. They were holding on to their old ways, their old lives, and their old desires rather than dying to those desires and obediently following the Lord's leading. They were looking in their rearview mirrors at something that should have been completely dead: their former lives in a slave nation.

Because the children of Israel hadn't died to themselves and followed God's leading with all their hearts, what should have been a two-week journey wound up taking forty years. As a result, a whole generation of Israelites died in the wilderness...without claiming for themselves what God had promised them.

In the New Testament, the apostle Paul tells us very directly not to be complainers: "Do everything without complaining or arguing, so that you may become blameless and pure, children of God without fault in a crooked and depraved generation, in which you shine like stars in the universe" (Philippians 2:14–15, NIV).

So why does God sometimes allow us to remain in confusing life situations where He places us?

My friend, it's all about His glory.

When you and I display peace, persistence, and confidence in the midst of perplexing circumstances, our lives stand out, and people take notice. Griping is a way of life for most people, and when we refuse to participate, it says that there is something different in our lives. Something supernatural. And we get to tell them what it's all about.

This doesn't mean that we can't say we're hurting when we're hurting, sick when we're sick, and confused when we're confused. What it means is that when we admit those things—to ourselves, to our spouses and families, to outsiders, and of course to God—we're acknowledging in the very next breath that we're submitted to the will of God, even when we don't fully understand what He's doing with us.

THOMAS'S TWIN

John tells us that Thomas had another name: Dydymus, which means "twin." Evidently, he had a twin brother or sister somewhere, though that person is never identified in Scripture.

Part of the reason that fact caught my eye is because of a pair of identical twins who attend weekly morning services at our church.

You literally can't tell these two people apart (unless you know them *very* well) because they look alike, talk alike, walk alike, and worship the same God alike.

I am told that this is hardly unusual for twins. They very often take on the same looks, emotional and mental attributes, speech patterns, and other characteristics, simply because their life experiences are identical.

As I thought about how twins are often so much alike, it occurred to me that there is a challenge hidden between the lines of John's text, telling us that Thomas was also called "twin." Here it is: Are you willing to be Thomas's twin? Are you willing to so deeply and completely trust Jesus Christ that you will do what He says to do, say what He wants you to say, and go where He wants you to go...even when His directions seem confusing...*especially* when they seem confusing?

Jesus' call to follow Him even at the risk of death wasn't just for the twelve apostles, but to all of His disciples. That includes that guy or gal you saw in the mirror this morning! And when we die to ourselves and submit our will to His, He will take us to a place where we'll see miracles in the making. Life out of death! That's the decision Thomas made when Jesus said, "Let's go...." And because he obeyed, even in the face of personal risk and danger, he was never again the same.

God cares when you're confused, when the situations and events in your life seem to make no sense, and when what He is saying to you has you completely baffled. He cares…but the fact is He often arranges circumstances in our lives to cause us some confusion. When that happens, you can count on the fact that He's working behind the scenes to mold you into the kind of believer He wants all of us to be: one that focuses on the spiritual, one with a strong and growing faith, and one who is committed to following Him and obeying Him in every step of your walk with Him.

4

God, Do You Really Care...

WHEN I'M HURTING?

There may be no greater pain on earth than that which comes with the death of a loved one. Yes, there are plenty of other hurts to go around. We ache over bruised or broken relationships. We grieve over unfulfilled goals and dreams, and countless other disappointments in life.

But death—be it the death of parent, sibling, spouse, child, or dear friend—hurts even more profoundly, mostly because it's so final.

You would think it would be different for those of us who rest in the hope of heaven—who know our saved loved one is in a far, far better place. And it is. As the Scripture says, don't "grieve as do the rest who have no hope" (1 Thessalonians 4:13).

But it still hurts.

Our loved one may be in heaven, but *we* aren't. We're still on this side of eternity, with all its loneliness, sorrows, and pain. And when someone we love so much slips away to the other side, we miss them terribly. We know we'll never see that individual again in this life.

John's account of the story of Lazarus of Bethany gives us examples of how so many of us might respond when we lose someone near and dear to us. As Jesus arrived in Bethany, His dear friends Mary and Martha were obviously rocked with pain and fresh grief over the loss of their brother.

What made it so much worse was that it was a loss they believed would never happen! The Lord Himself had sent them a message that their brother's sickness wouldn't end in death.

It's one thing to try to absorb the enormous shock of losing our loved one, but it's a whole other level of pain when we feel so sure we'd heard the voice of God telling us that things would turn out all right—that our loved one wouldn't die.

By the time Jesus finally arrived in town, Lazarus had been in the tomb for four days. To the grieving sisters, this late arrival must have seemed like a broken promise—and like one big contradiction.

Lazarus was dead. And what's worse, Jesus had let them down. The pain must have been unbearable.

In chapter 1, I pointed out that God doesn't always come immediately to the rescue when we're in a time of need, but that He always sends us a personal word. But what do we do when it seems that the word we have received contradicts the reality in our lives? When it seems that God has failed to keep a personal promise? When it seems that this God who identifies Himself as the personification of love and compassion has contradicted Himself and let us down?

As odd as it may sound—and as difficult as it may be to do when we are suffering—those are the very times when we need to focus on our God and His love for us more than ever. Why? Because it may well be that He's about to do something for us beyond all our expectations. After pleading with Him for an *A* or *B*—or possibly *C*—He comes walking in through the back door with *Z*. And we say, "I could have never imagined or predicted *that!*"

HOW DOES HE KNOW?

When you're hurting for whatever reason, you need to hold fast to the fact that Jesus knows and cares about your pain. "But how?" you may be asking. "How does Jesus know?" He demonstrated that very clearly in the story we've been considering in this book.

Two days after He had received word that his dear friend had fallen deathly ill, Jesus said to the disciples, "Our friend Lazarus has fallen asleep; but I go, so that I may awaken him out of sleep" (John

11:11). By now, we all know that Jesus was speaking figuratively. When their faces reflected total confusion, He told them very plainly, "Lazarus is dead, and I am glad for your sakes that I was not there, so that you may believe; but let us go to him" (vv. 14–15).

Jesus knew Lazarus had died, and He knew Mary and Martha were hurting because of it. But how did He know? He hadn't gone to Bethany since He'd received the news that Lazarus was sick, and there is no record of further communication after that.

Jesus wasn't physically with Mary and Martha, yet He knew what had happened and knew they were grieving. And He knew those things for one reason: Jesus was so in tune and in touch with His Father that He was able to see through the miles that physically separated Him from His dear friends.

The same is true for us today when we're in deep pain.

The Bible tells us that after Jesus' death and resurrection, He returned to heaven, where He took His seat at the right hand of the Father (see Acts 2:33, Hebrews 1:3). But the Word also tells us that He doesn't just sit there observing the happenings of our lives from afar, but stays busy interceding for us, pleading our case before God (see Romans 8:34).

Jesus knows when we're hurting over the loss of a loved one, knows when our hearts ache over personal failures or broken relationships. He knows when we're sad, when we feel misunderstood, when we've been devastated because someone has said or done something that is patently wrong and unfair.

The key question all of us need answered is: If Jesus knows about our pain, why does He sometimes delay in taking care of those things that have us hurting?

WHY THE DELAY?

Although it's hard for us to grasp in this era of cell phones, pagers, and instant messaging, it's highly possible that Lazarus had already died by the time Jesus received word of his illness. Perea was about thirty miles from Bethany, and it wasn't until two days had passed that Jesus and the disciples began their journey back to Bethany. By the time they arrived, Mary and Martha already considered the situation closed. Lazarus was gone. Jesus hadn't come. Life had to go on.

What's important in this story, however, isn't the timing of Lazarus's death or of Jesus' arrival in Bethany, but the *intention* behind Jesus' delayed response. As we read this account, what jumps out at us is that Jesus had a purpose for His delay.

He always does.

Mary and Martha had put out a first-century 911 call. It was an emergency needing attention *right now*, or "STAT," as they say in the emergency room. The sisters knew their brother would die if something wasn't done, and they did the one thing they knew beyond any doubt could help him: they called for Jesus.

But Jesus didn't just drop everything and head for Bethany. Instead, He sent the sisters a message of comfort and assurance, then stayed put for two more days. By the time He left Perea, Lazarus was certainly dead. But that, it turns out, was part of God's plan for the glorification of the Son.

This is not a case of someone being caught off guard or miscalculating the situation. This was an example of a Savior who cares deeply when His people are hurting, but who has a plan to teach us and expand our faith in the very midst of our pain.

SAME PAIN, DIFFERENT EXPRESSIONS

As you read of Mary and Martha in the Gospels, it becomes fairly obvious that these two women—while they both had tremendous faith in and love for Jesus—were "wired" very differently. That is evident in how they responded to Jesus when He finally arrived at the outskirts of Bethany: "Martha therefore, when she heard that Jesus was coming, went to meet Him, but Mary stayed at the house" (John 11:20).

There are some Bible verses I read and immediately understand what God is saying to me through them. But there are others I can *feel.* John 11:20 is one of the latter. When I read it, I can just *feel* Mary's disappointment over the death of her brother. But I can also feel her disappointment with Jesus Himself. Mary had believed with all her heart that her brother wouldn't die, and that Jesus would show up in time to heal him. Now, with her brother in the grave four days, she couldn't even summon what it took to go outside her house and face the dearest person in her life.

Have you ever felt that way toward God? Have you ever wanted to say to Him, "If You had only stepped in sooner, then I wouldn't be feeling this pain"? Have you ever felt as though God let you down and abandoned you when you needed Him most? Worse yet, have you ever believed that you heard a personal word from God— a Bible-confirmed message just to you—only to find that what you believed you heard didn't come to pass?

That was what Mary grappled with as Jesus arrived in Bethany. But we will see as we continue on in this story that Jesus cares when we are hurting, even when—maybe *especially* when—we are in such pain that we can't even approach Him to talk about it.

PAIN AND A PERSONAL WORD

In chapter 1, we talked about God's kindness and care in sending us a personal word in our times of sickness and distress—a message just for us through the Holy Spirit's illumination of His written Word.

We need to remember that when God sends us a personal word, we can count on Him to keep it. And He keeps His word to us when He comes to us personally and *shows* us how much He cares as He ministers to us in our pain.

He may not show up when we expect Him to.

He may not show up in the way we expect Him to.

But He will always show up on time...not our time, maybe, but the right time.

Jesus demonstrated this principle in Mary and Martha's situation. Though at first He ministered to them through a word only, it was just a matter of timing as to when He would arrive on the scene and tend to His dear friends' situation in a tangible and personal way.

When Jesus first arrived near Bethany, the first thing Martha and Mary did was register a complaint: "Lord, if You had been here, my brother would not have died" (John 11:21, 32). The way I read this, it wasn't just a complaint, but also an accusation. In effect, they were saying, "Our brother wouldn't be dead now if You had just come when we called You!"

The fact that Martha and Mary both registered the same complaint with Jesus tells me that in the four days prior to Jesus' arrival in Bethany—the same four days their brother had been wrapped in a shroud and sealed in a tomb—they had been talking about their feelings with one another. Hurt and anger had to have been part of that conversation.

But what stands out to me most in this scene isn't Mary and Martha's complaints. They were just doing what so many believers do when they're in pain: blame God. ("If He's such a loving God, how could He allow me to suffer so much?") What really strikes me about this scene is Jesus' response.

Silence.

In my own human thinking, it's easy for me to imagine Jesus listening to Mary and Martha's accusations, then sternly rebuking and correcting the two women. I can just hear Him saying, "Just who do you think you're talking to? Don't you know who I am? I am God's chosen One, and I have prerogatives of where to go and when to go there."

Yet Jesus didn't respond directly to these complaints. He didn't chide or correct them but simply went about comforting them…and preparing them for the miracle He was about to do on their behalf.

But why didn't Jesus correct Mary and Martha? I believe it was because He knew what was really in their hearts.

An understanding friend knows our hearts. He or she knows that when we're hurting, we may say things we might not otherwise say. A friend like that is able to see through our words into our pain, and feel that pain with us.

I believe that's what was happening as Jesus listened to Mary and Martha expressing their disappointment. Jesus knew these women loved Him dearly. He knew that their words weren't coming from what was really in their hearts toward Him.

It was just their grief talking.

JESUS RESPONDS

Arriving near Bethany, Jesus was greeted by a scene of incredible hurt and disappointment. Both Martha and Mary were hurting and angry, and they were joined in their grieving by what was probably a sizeable group of Jews who had come to mourn with them. Eventually (and I'll get to this in more detail later) Mary came out of her home to see Jesus, and the first thing she did was fall at His feet, weeping.

And what was Jesus' response to all the pain and grieving? John tells us, "When Jesus therefore saw her weeping, and the Jews who came with her also weeping, He was deeply moved in spirit, *and was troubled*" (John 11:33).

We can easily understand the "moved in spirit" part. When Jesus saw and felt the huge wave of pain and sorrow rolling out from that scene, it moved Him. Yes, Jesus was the Son of God, but He was also a man who felt the same kinds of emotions we feel. There was no way He could be at a scene like this and not be emotionally touched.

But there was something more here.

Jesus wasn't just moved in spirit but also "troubled." In the original language, the word *troubled* can also be read as "disturbed" or "shaken," suggesting that Jesus was seeing something beyond the grief and tears.

With His heart still troubled and disturbed, Jesus asked the mourners where Lazarus was buried. As they all made their way toward the tomb, the people could easily see that Jesus was touched by what was going on around Him, and the shortest verse in the Bible tells us why: "Jesus wept" (John 11:35).

When the Jewish mourners saw Jesus crying, many of them naturally assumed it was for the same reason everyone else was weeping: because He loved Lazarus and was grieving over his death. But this was much more than weeping over the loss of a friend.

Others at the gravesite saw something else in Jesus' tears. John tells us: "But some of them said, 'Could not this man, who opened the eyes of the blind man, have kept this man also from dying?'" (11:37). In other words, some might have believed Jesus was crying because He was helpless—because there was nothing He could do for a man already dead. And Jesus wouldn't have missed the implication of their words: If He couldn't keep Lazarus from dying in the first place, then maybe He's not everything people say He is.

Over the centuries, people have attempted to explain the reason for Jesus' tears in this scene. Some have held that He was moved in spirit and weeping simply because He so deeply sympathized with the grief of those around Him. That theory has some merit... but there's another explanation we need to consider.

Throughout His ministry, Jesus had never responded this way in the face of human suffering and grief. Although Jesus had already been at several scenes of death, unspeakable suffering, and deeply felt pain, His response had not been to cry, but to roll up His sleeves to heal and raise the dead.

While I firmly believe that Jesus was moved with emotion because of what was happening in the lives of these two women, I believe His tears were also motivated by something else, something no one—not Mary, not Martha, and not the mourners who had come to comfort them—could comprehend but Jesus Himself.

A DIFFERENT KIND OF GRIEF

The Gospels record two instances of Jesus weeping: outside Lazarus's tomb and as He looked out over the holy city of Jerusalem and wept over its lack of faith: "O Jerusalem, Jerusalem, you who kill the prophets and stone those sent to you, how often I have longed to gather your children together, as a hen gathers her chicks under her wings, but you were not willing" (Matthew 23:37, NIV).

This was Jesus crying tears of grief, but not because He was mourning over the loss of a loved one. These were tears over a people who had turned their backs on God, who refused to receive what He had long ago promised and offered to them. Jesus was grieved to His very core for one reason: The people of Israel were rejecting God's chosen One.

I believe His tears in the scene outside Lazarus's grave were motivated in part by the very same feelings.

As the moment approached for Jesus to bring Lazarus back from the dead, He gave the command to have the stone rolled away from the grave. Again, a grieving Martha protested, pointing out the obvious: "Lord, by this time there will be a stench, for he has been dead four days" (John 11:39).

Martha, though she had already had a very intense spiritual conversation with Jesus just outside of town, was still thinking in the natural. She still hadn't reconciled her brother's death with the Lord's promise that his illness would not end in death. It *had* ended in death! How could you get around it?

When we read Jesus' response to Martha, He sounds more than a little peeved that she doesn't understand that something miraculous and spectacular is about to happen. "Did I not say," Jesus told her, "if you believe, you will see the glory of God?" (John 11:40). When I read, "Did I not say…?" I can't help but think of a good scolding along the lines of, "How many times do I have to tell you…?" or "If you'd just pay attention, you'd know that…"

I believed Jesus was disturbed and troubled at the grief and crying on the scene not just because of the natural human emotions, but because the tears of grief weren't mixed with tears of faith. He saw people that day who were so controlled by their circumstances that they couldn't grasp what He had already told them—that God would be glorified that day!

If you've ever been to a memorial or funeral for a man or woman of faith, you can see the contrasts in how people express their grief. Those who can't make a spiritual connection between their sorrow and the person who has passed away will feel nothing but loss. To them, it's all dust and ashes. Their friend is simply dead and they will never see that person again.

Those who know Jesus Christ personally will cry tears and feel sorrow, too. They will grieve because their loved one won't be there for them anymore—and they will miss that person. But behind all that there will be an air of calmness and comfort—you can sense it when you're near them! They know that the death of their friend doesn't mean the end of their friend. Yes, they're wounded and gripped with grief. But they're also greatly comforted in the knowledge that physical death isn't the end, but actually the beginning of eternal life in the presence of Jesus Christ.

They know beyond all doubt that they will see their friend, their loved one, again. As the apostle Paul wrote:

> Listen, I tell you a mystery: We will not all sleep, but we will all be changed—in a flash, in the twinkling of an eye, at the last trumpet. For the trumpet will sound, the dead will be raised imperishable, and we will be changed. For the perishable must clothe itself with the imperishable, and the mortal with immortality. When the perishable has been clothed with the imperishable, and the mortal with immortality,

then the saying that is written will come true: "Death has been swallowed up in victory." "Where, O death, is your victory? Where, O death, is your sting?"

1 CORINTHIANS 15:51–55, NIV

Jesus wasn't troubled *only* because the people around Him were in pain and crying. He was troubled because their tears reflected a lack of faith in what He had already told them. In other words, they were focused on what had caused their pain—the death of Lazarus—and not on the One who had come to defeat death for Lazarus and his sisters that day...and for the rest of us when He gave Himself up to die for our sins.

There's nothing at all wrong with us allowing ourselves to feel pain when we lose a loved one—or for any number of other reasons. In fact, I would say there is something wrong with us if we don't. But when we know Jesus Christ and know that He cares and will be there for us in the midst of our pain, there will be an element of trust and joy in our tears. We know that Jesus Christ will keep every promise He has ever made.

GRIEVING OVER DEATH ITSELF

There is another reason Jesus wept outside Lazarus's tomb, one no doubt lost on everyone else at the scene. And it was this: Jesus saw up close and personal the effects of death, and it grieved Him that His loved one, Lazarus, had to go through it.

Death can come to us in a multiplicity of ways—through disease, accident, old age, and countless others—but ultimately there is one thing that puts us in the grave: sin. The Bible tells us that it was through Adam's sin that death was passed on to all of humanity. That means many things, but one big thing each of us must face: We will all die physically someday.

One day, Jesus will completely and thoroughly eradicate physical death, but in the meantime, He's already taken care of spiritual death for all who believe in Him. If you believe that Jesus Christ is the Son of God and came to provide you with forgiveness of sin and eternal life, if you place your trust in Him, and make Him your Leader and Lord, then you will live eternally. That's because the thing that brought you death in the first place—sin—has been addressed. Because sin has been addressed, when you die physically you step immediately into the presence of the Lord. You'll be swept up into life everlasting so fast that you won't be dead enough to attend your own funeral!

Death is the hallmark of Satan. The devil's whole plan in bringing sin into the world in the first place was so that he could bring death of all kinds to those in God's creation. But when Jesus Christ called Lazarus from the grave, He overruled the devil and the curse that put Lazarus in the grave in the first place.

No one could do that but God Himself.

When you're hurting, it's because some*one* or some*thing* in your life has died. It might be a loved one or a dear friend, or it might be a dream or a goal you've set for yourself. But Jesus has sent all of us who believe in Him a word, and that word is this: "I have defeated death once and for all."

Jesus cared so deeply and profoundly that His children had to experience the pain of death that He cried tears of grief over it, right along with the grieving crowd around him.

But that wasn't the end of the story, was it?

It isn't the end of the story in our lives either. Jesus cares when we're hurting over death. We know that's true because He's told us so. But we can also believe that He will put action behind His words and tears. He will step into the middle of our pain and grief over death and do something miraculous.

5

God, Do You Really Care...
WHEN I'M DISAPPOINTED?

Is disappointment losing something good you expected, or experiencing something bad you didn't expect at all?

It may be a little of both. Either way, it hurts.

Taking it a step further, we might say that disappointment is the pain we experience when something we've been holding on to dies. It could be the death of a loved one, but it could also be the death of a vision, the death of a dream, or the death of our hopes for the fulfillment of a promise.

I think it's safe to say that every believer has had something die in his or her life and felt the devastating letdown that follows. And in the wake of such crushing disappointment, we find ourselves asking, *God, where were You in all this?*

That's a query common to all humankind, and it's the very question both Martha and Mary asked Jesus when He finally arrived near the village of Bethany...four days after the death of their brother Lazarus.

JESUS, WHERE WERE YOU?

When Jesus finally arrived in Bethany, disappointment hung in the air like L.A. smog. John tells us that a crowd of Jewish people had made the two-mile trek from Jerusalem to Bethany to console and comfort Mary and Martha.

Into the midst of all this wailing and tears came Jesus.

Yes, the Master had arrived. But too late to help.

Or so they thought.

Losing their brother when Jesus had distinctly said that his sickness would *not* end in death was a devastating blow for Mary and Martha. The sisters' responses to Jesus revealed the disappointment that permeated their grief.

When Martha heard that Jesus was nearing Bethany, she ran out to meet Him. "Lord," she said, "if You had been here my brother would not have died" (John 11:21). Mary said the same thing a few minutes later.

Those who are disappointed and hurting often use "If only" statements. "*If only* I had..." or "*If only* he had..." or "*If only* it hadn't happened this way...." Statements such as these reflect the belief that if someone had made another choice or turned another way, or if circumstances had taken a turn to the left instead of the right, then a particular situation would have turned out differently.

Both of these women wanted an answer to one simple question: *Where had Jesus been when they needed Him?* They knew that their brother had been deathly sick and that they had called out to Jesus for help. But the hours and days slipped by, Jesus never showed up, and Lazarus drew his last rattling breath, and died.

Jesus had waited two more days in Perea before coming to see them. That hurt! The two women had deep disappointment that hovered on the edge of being *bitter* disappointment.

WHO'S TO BLAME?

When Mary and Martha said to Jesus, "If You had been here, my brother would not have died," what they were really saying was, "This is Your fault, Jesus, because we called You knowing that You could have kept Lazarus alive, but You did nothing to help us."

Those of us who have been through a situation where we felt bitter disappointment know that this is a time when our true feelings tend to rise to the surface. In times like these, we're less likely to weigh our words. We're hurting, and the hurt sometimes comes pouring out of our mouths.

There is a touch of anger in Martha and Mary's words—and maybe a little bitterness as well. They both got right at the heart of what they were feeling that day, and it wasn't pretty. In essence, they were telling Jesus that He had let them down—at the very time when they needed Him so desperately.

As I pointed out earlier, Mary and Martha weren't the only ones to voice their disappointment. Some of the Jewish people who had come to comfort and console them—probably including some of Jesus' enemies—expressed their own cynical brand of disappointment: "Could not this man, who opened the eyes of the blind man, have kept this man also from dying?" (John 11:37).

But there was a profound difference between the way Mary and Martha expressed their disappointment and the way some of the mourners did.

WHERE TO BRING YOUR DISAPPOINTMENT

Do you believe that disappointment—even bitter disappointment—and faith can exist in the same heart? Can the two commingle? Can they produce blessings such as a strengthened faith and deeper relationship with God?

Sounds like a bit of a stretch, doesn't it?

In fact, disappointment and faith might coexist better than you would have imagined.

Do you believe that God is okay with your expressions of disappointment? Does He care enough when you are disappointed to listen to you, speak to you, gently reason with you, and comfort you as you pour out your pain-filled heart before Him? Or is it better to keep your disappointment to yourself—sealed up tightly inside a smooth religious veneer?

Obviously Martha was disappointed—disappointed that their little family had been torn apart by death, and disappointed with their Friend, Jesus. But we need to take note of where she took those feelings: To Jesus Himself! There were plenty of mourners around that week who would have sympathized with her and shared their own doubts and disappointments about Jesus.

But she didn't go to those people.

She just took it all to Jesus, laying it at His feet.

Martha's words reflect both her disappointment and her faith in Jesus and the Father. In one breath she says, "If You had been here, my brother would not have died," but in the very next breath she acknowledges, "Even now I know that whatever You ask of God, God will give You" (John 11:22).

While Martha was disappointed with Jesus—as well as angry and maybe even bitter—she went straight to Him simply because she knew who He really was.

Even as Martha spilled out her heart, telling the Lord how let down she felt, she also affirmed her faith in Jesus. The mourners noted Jesus' arrival, too. But they voiced their grief in a completely different way, basically questioning whether Jesus was all He had claimed to be.

And how did Jesus react?

He responded to Martha's disappointment by conversing with her, giving her comfort and assurance, and leading her into a deeper faith in Him. Conversely, He had nothing to say to those Jews on the scene that doubted Him and questioned His credentials.

When your faith is firmly in Jesus Christ, you don't need to hide your anger, hurt, or disappointment from Him. After all, He knows what you're thinking and feeling anyway, and He will never reject you for pouring out those emotions percolating in your soul.

Part of life on this earth is going through disappointments over death—the death of a vision, the death of a dream, or the physical death of a loved one. Sometimes the disappointment and pain over those kinds of losses can be so deep and so consuming that we can't help but cry out to God and ask Him if He really cares. But even at our lowest points in life, we can be assured of two things.

First, we can be assured that God cares when we are disappointed. He loves us with a love far wider and deeper than anything we can imagine, and when we are hurting, He feels it with us and seeks to comfort us. The psalmist tells us: "The LORD is near to the brokenhearted and saves those who are crushed in spirit" (Psalm 34:18).

But there is a second assurance in this story. As we communicate with Him honestly and openly about our disappointments, telling Him our sorrow and despair, we can be assured that we love and serve a Savior who has the Father's ear. And He's a Father who will give Jesus anything He asks for.

Martha demonstrated that kind of faith, and before this scene was over, Jesus would give her what she had asked for in the first place—even if it didn't happen in the way she had expected. He would give her something infinitely more amazing than a healing for her brother.

He would give her a resurrection.

RESTING IN THE FAITH OF ANOTHER

Martha had told Jesus, "I know that whatever You ask of God, God will give You." In saying that, she was not only acknowledging who Jesus was and who God was, but also the perfect relationship between them.

The Father and the Son have always lived in perfect relationship. While Jesus ministered on earth, He was completely committed to doing the will of the Father and *only* the will of the Father. At the same time, the Father was committed to the authority He had given the Son—to do and say the things God wanted us to see and hear.

Martha understood this perfect Father-Son relationship, and she understood that in her time of deep disappointment—a time when her faith could very well have been shaken to its core—she could go to Jesus and "piggyback" on *His* perfect faith. She knew that Jesus was in perfect harmony with His Father and that nothing He asked for would ever be turned down from above.

If that seems like a stretch or like I'm reading more into this account than what God really has to say, then note what the apostle Paul declared concerning this aspect of faith: "This was in accordance with the eternal purpose which He carried out in Christ Jesus our Lord, in whom we have boldness and confident access *through faith in Him*" (Ephesians 3:11–12).

Even at first reading, that looks like a great promise, doesn't it? It essentially says that we can have bold and confident assurance that we as God's children have access to Him simply because we have faith in Jesus Christ. But in some versions of the Bible, this verse contains a note giving us the literal rendering, which is "through the faith of Him" or "through His faith."

I believe that's what the passage teaches here.

What Paul is actually telling us is that we can have confidence in Jesus' faith, a perfect faith, a faith that has complete confidence that the Father will grant Him anything and everything He requests.

I'M DISAPPOINTED, BUT *I KNOW*...

When Martha acknowledged Jesus' identity and His relationship with the Father, she began with the phrase *I know*. Martha was in a situation where she was sure of very little...except Jesus' relationship with the Father. The only thing she really knew for sure was that her brother was dead and that there was nothing she could do to change that fact. But as Martha looked outside her present situation, if only for a moment, she was able to state with absolute confidence who Jesus was and what the Father would do for Him.

Decades after this scene, as John wrote his first letter, he declared that we can have confidence in this relationship as we pray:

> These things I have written to you who believe in the name of the Son of God, so that you may know that you have eternal life. This is the confidence which we have before Him, that, if we ask anything according to His will, He hears us. And if we know that He hears us in whatever we ask, we know that we have the requests which we have asked from Him.
>
> 1 JOHN 5:13–15

John is telling us that when we talk to God, we can be absolutely confident that He hears us simply because we come to

Him in the name of Jesus Christ. And why can we do this? Because, John tells us, we believe in the name of the Son of God.

Most believers in our culture end their prayers with words such as, "In Jesus' name, Amen." But what does it mean to pray in Jesus' name? This has to be more than just a nice-sounding tagline to our prayers to make them "extra religious."

When we pray "in Jesus' name," we are actually claiming the authority of Jesus Christ Himself in our prayers. We're applying the same kind of "I know" faith Martha showed when she acknowledged Jesus' relationship with the Father. When we pray about our disappointment and pain in our Lord's name, we are essentially saying to Him, "I need You to back me up on this, Jesus, because I'm not sure I'm getting through. I'm too frustrated, too angry, too weak, too broken, and too confused to know if my prayers are making it past the ceiling. But I know above all this that the Father will never turn You down."

Have you ever been in a situation where you needed or wanted to gain access to an event reserved for a specific group of people, but didn't have the authority to get in? If so, you may have discovered that it's sometimes possible to gain admittance through the authority of another.

Suppose, for example, you wanted to go to a concert, limited to an exclusive group of invitees. You call everyone you know who might be going in an attempt to get in the concert hall the night of the event, but no dice. Finally, someone you know who has a pass to the event calls and tells you, "I can't make it to the concert, but I'd like you to have my pass. It has my name on it, but I'll call and make sure they let you in when you show my pass at the door."

In that situation, you would basically be piggybacking on the name of someone else in order to go to the concert you'd wanted so badly to see. Without that name, you couldn't even get through the door, but with it, you are afforded all the perks and privileges reserved for the original holder of the pass. And all that simply because you know the person who was well-connected enough to have received an exclusive invitation.

In the same way, those of us who know and love Jesus Christ have a personal relationship with the One who has all the perks and privileges of a perfect relationship with God the Father. And because of that, we have access to the Father through the faith of the Son.

Talk about amazing grace!

In the midst of what might have been the darkest time of her life, Martha appealed to what she knew to be true: that Jesus was the Son of God and that the Father gave Him what He requested. Because of that, she knew deep in her heart that her situation and her circumstances wouldn't have the final word that day. She couldn't know for sure what Jesus would ask for, but she knew that whatever it was, God would do it for Him…and for her.

JESUS GETS THE LAST WORD

In the grip of grief and perplexity, Martha was somehow able to acknowledge Jesus' identity and His perfect relationship with the Father. As a result, she received yet another personal word from the lips of God's Son. And this time, it was face to face.

"Your brother will rise again" (John 11:23).

Martha knew her scripture. Looking up into the Lord's face, she responded, "I know that he will rise again in the resurrection on the last day."

Most Jews—excluding the unhappy Sadducee party—believed in an end-times resurrection. The Pharisees, the dominant sect in the Jewish religious leadership at that time, believed in and taught the scriptural fact of the resurrection. Jewish boys of the time were required to undergo years of Bible teaching and study. Although Martha had probably not undergone that kind of study, she was aware of the teaching of the end-time resurrection and understood that her brother—as well as all other believers—would one day be raised from the dead.

Taken by itself, Jesus' promise that Lazarus would rise again could have been heard as a strong word of encouragement in the midst of Martha's struggle. It would be much like a modern-day believer telling a brother or sister in Christ that his or her saved friend or loved one is now "in a better place," specifically in the presence of the Lord.

That's a wonderful truth, and there's no denying it. It's a fact that can make all the difference to a grieving believer mourning the loss of a loved one.

But Jesus had something even more for Martha that day.

IT'S *WHO* YOU KNOW

Jesus didn't correct Martha when she acknowledged the final resurrection. After all, she was speaking biblical truth! Instead, He took her a step further in her faith telling her, "I am the resurrection and the life; he who believes in Me will live even if he dies, and everyone who lives and believes in Me will never die. Do you believe this?" (John 11:25–26).

Martha had already gone partway to where Jesus wanted to take her. She had already spoken sound and right doctrine when she acknowledged that there would be a resurrection for all believers at the end of time. But Jesus wanted to draw a distinction for Martha—and for us—between doctrine and the *person* of Jesus Christ. In essence, He is telling her that her belief in the resurrection was a sound and right one but that *He* was the resurrection. The reason her brother would rise from the dead was because *He* had said so.

Of course, sound biblical teaching holds a vital place in the life of every believer. We've got to know *what* we believe and *why* we believe it.

The apostle Paul wrote to a young preacher named Timothy about the importance of believing and preaching sound doctrine: "In pointing out these things to the brethren, you will be a good servant of Christ Jesus, constantly nourished on the words of the faith and of the sound doctrine which you have been following" (1 Timothy 4:6). Later on in the very same letter, Paul told Timothy, "If anyone advocates a different doctrine and does not agree with sound words, those of our Lord Jesus Christ, and with the doctrine conforming to godliness, he is conceited and understands nothing" (1 Timothy 6:3-4).

But as important as solid teaching is, we can't get so stuck on it that we miss the person of Jesus Christ. That would be as foolish as being so focused on a medical book that we miss the doctor, so focused on the law that we miss the lawyer, so focused on the penal code that we miss the importance of the police officer, so focused on the composition of the atmosphere that we forget to breathe. If we remain stuck on knowing doctrine without knowing Jesus as the personification of all truth, we won't be prepared for those inevitable times in life when the roof falls in and the ground shakes beneath our feet. But when we acknowledge who He really is, we will receive the comfort and blessings we seek.

But there is a condition to that, and it's this: our confession has to be verbal.

"DO YOU BELIEVE THIS?"

It was a pointed question, and it needed a direct answer.

Looking steadily into Martha's tear-stained face, Jesus had said, "I am the resurrection and the life; he who believes in Me will live even if he dies, and everyone who lives and believes in Me will never die."

Those were the facts. And Jesus wanted Martha to respond to those facts.

"Do you believe this?"

The answer had to be yes or no. There was no room for bobbing and weaving. There was no room for a political answer that said both or neither, like something from the lips of a presidential candidate dodging a reporter's query on *Meet the Press*.

Everything was in place for Jesus to perform an awesome miracle. But before that physical miracle of raising Lazarus from the dead would take place, Jesus wanted to do an inner miracle in the heart of His friend Martha. He wanted to see her move forward from mere book and head knowledge to a more personal, living faith.

"Do you believe this?"

Now if you have read the Gospels, you know that Jesus often led people into knowledge and faith by asking questions. Sometimes those questions were responses to questions people had asked Him, and sometimes they were designed to lead people from surface knowledge to real faith.

When Jesus asked Martha if she believed that He was the resurrection and that everyone who believes in Him would live forever, it wasn't just rhetorical. He expected an answer. He wanted Martha to verbalize what she believed, not to be silent about it.

And Martha did respond.

Without missing a beat, she replied, "Yes, Lord; I have believed that You are the Christ, the Son of God, even He who comes into the world" (John 11:27).

Martha's confession is almost identical to one from the lips of Simon Peter. Jesus had just asked the disciples what others were saying about Him. They responded by telling Him that some believed He was John the Baptist, while others thought He was the second coming of Elijah. Still others believed he was one of the Old Testament prophets raised from the dead.

So much for theory. So much for religious talk.

Jesus turned to those men and made the question intensely personal—as He will for every one of us. "But who do *you* say I am?"

Peter, the one who always spoke up and acted when the others were too timid to say anything, answered, "You are the Christ, the Son of the living God" (Matthew 16:16).

The big fisherman got it right. And Jesus' response to Peter's verbal declaration tells us a lot about the importance of proclaiming the identity of Jesus Christ with our mouths: "*Blessed are you*, Simon Barjona, because flesh and blood did not reveal this to you, but My Father who is in heaven" (Matthew 16:17).

The real key to any kind of blessing from God is to verbally acknowledge who Jesus Christ really is: the Son of God. The all-powerful Second Person of the Trinity. And when we are disappointed and hurting, we have an opportunity to experience a "right now" kind of God, not just a God who blesses us in "the sweet by-and-by." But in order to receive a blessing from Him, we must be willing to acknowledge Him. Not just in our heads, not just in our hearts, but with our mouths.

Martha wasn't going to get her miracle that day until she was able to verbally acknowledge Jesus' relationship with the Father and His true identity. And why? Because God honors those who honor the Son through their words. Jesus said, "Therefore everyone who confesses Me before men, I will also confess him before My Father who is in heaven. But whoever denies Me before men, I will also deny him before My Father who is in heaven" (Matthew 10:32–33).

When we read those words, we usually take them to refer to the end time's judgment, when every man and woman who has pro-claimed Jesus Christ will receive their eternal reward. There's nothing wrong with that reading of the passage, but I also believe it has a more immediate, "in-this-life" meaning behind it.

When we go to God in prayer, we are to go in the name of Jesus. We do this because He is our advocate with the Father, and what-ever we request in His name will be done for us, as long as it's within God's will. In other words, Jesus is the One who "signs off" on any-thing we request of God. And when we verbally confess Jesus Christ as our Lord and Savior, He is more than willing to confess us before the Father and give us what we request. But when we fail to do that, He has to deny us before the Father, and that includes our requests.

When we are hurting and disappointed, when something has died in our lives and left us feeling as though our world is falling apart, *our first response to Jesus should be to acknowledge who He really is.* My friend, there is power in declaring who He is and what He has done and can do. Who is He? He is the one and only Son of God who receives anything and everything He requests of the Father. When we do that, He is free to comfort us in our pain and give us perspective in our disappointments.

And more than that.

He'll perform a resurrection.

The great nineteenth-century American evangelist Dwight L. Moody once said, "Trust in yourself, and you are doomed to disappointment; trust in your friends, and they will die and leave you; trust in money, and you may have it taken from you; trust in reputation, and some slanderous tongue may blast it; but trust in God, and you are never to be confounded in time or eternity."

Our God is the One we can trust to enter personally into the bruised tissue of our soul. One we can count on to care when our friends, our family, and our personal reputations all fail us. When we put our trust in Him, He will never allow us to continue on blindly in our disappointment, but will instead teach us more about the meaning of real faith.

Jesus knew Martha and Mary were disappointed—bitterly so. He also knew that they had much to learn in the midst of their disappointment. Though they didn't realize it in the turmoil of their sorrow, He had a plan to turn that disappointment into praise.

This is a God who cares when we are disappointed...even when the disappointment is in Him.

6

God, Do You Really Care...
WHEN I CRY?

I recently talked with a young woman in the midst of some heart-wrenching struggles. She had been deeply disappointed that God hadn't come through for her as she believed He had promised.

Between the sobs and tears, she told me she was angry—angry at God, angry at people, even angry at me.

Angry at ME? What did I do?

It was nothing personal, she explained. She knew I'd done nothing to hurt or disappoint her. But she was deeply angry and disappointed at everything and everyone that had anything to do with God—and that included preachers.

It didn't take me long as I talked with this woman to see that she was hurting and frustrated—and just wanted someone to feel those feelings with her. But it also didn't take me long to realize that she was looking for hope. She truly *wanted* to believe that God really cared about her present situation. She *wanted* to believe that her emotional pain mattered to Him.

That's an important issue for all of us to address, isn't it? As believers, we know that God has made wonderful provision for us, both in the temporal and eternal sense. Still, we wonder, Does God really care when we're in such pain that we're moved to tears?

The answer to that question is a resounding, "Yes!"

Jesus demonstrated how much He cares about our tears by the way He interacted with Martha and Mary in the very heart of their sorrow.

TEARS

Humans are the only beings on earth who can enjoy a personal relationship with God. That's partly what the Bible means when it says God created us "in His image." Like our Creator, we have a mind, will, and emotions.

But there is something else unique to humans.

Tears.

Tears could indicate many different things in our lives.

Sometimes we shed tears of joy. I've conducted weddings where the waterworks started early and didn't stop until after the reception. Sometimes the bride starts the ball rolling. Standing at the altar and looking into the eyes of her beloved, a tear runs down her cheek. Before you know it, the whole place comes unglued and everybody's crying—the maids of honor, the groom, the families, the guests, the janitor, you name it.

While crying can sometimes be a demonstration of deep joy, it is more often an indication of something wrong in our lives. Most of the time when we see and hear someone crying, we can safely assume it's on account of hurt, disappointment, confusion, frustration, fear, anger, or any other number of negative human emotions.

Throughout this book, we've focused on two women in deep emotional pain—their lives turned upside down by the death of their beloved brother. When hopes are quenched, tears flow. They had hoped with all their hearts that Jesus would come. They had hoped that by this day, they would be dancing in joy with a healed and fully restored brother. But Lazarus was dead, and they simply could not explain what had happened to Jesus.

We remember Martha's words when she met Jesus just outside of town. "Lord, if you had been here, my brother would not have died" (John 11:21). Martha was certainly grieving, but her sister, Mary, couldn't even summon the will to leave the house and go meet Jesus.

Have you ever experienced pain that intense? Have you ever felt so hurt that you didn't even want to talk to God about it? So angry and disappointed that you wanted to stay away from other people—especially other Christians—and just wallow alone in your misery? So let down and disillusioned with God that you didn't want to hear about praying, fasting, or "drawing near"?

Most of us, if we were completely honest with ourselves, would have to admit to times when it feels better to just be alone in our misery than to get in the presence of God and His people. When we are angry, disappointed, or confused, it can be tempting to just shut ourselves away from God and to close our ears to anything He might have to say to us.

Most likely, that's just how Mary felt as she sat in her home *knowing* that Jesus was nearby. In her mind, He had let her down, and she just didn't have what it took to get up and go see Him—even though she knew how much He loved her. How could she escape the conclusion that Jesus could have done something, but didn't. Was it because He didn't care? I can just imagine that part of her heart said no, while part of her heart said, "Well...maybe."

Jesus, however, wasn't going to let Mary sit at home crying over the loss of her brother. He wanted her to come out of her home and come to Him. He wanted her to be in His presence as she cried. And why was that? Because He wanted to enter into her pain with her. He wanted to cry with her.

"THE TEACHER IS HERE...."

Jesus didn't chide or correct Martha when she complained to Him, "If You had been here..." Rather, He took the time to give her a clearer understanding of who He really was and what His identity meant to her. "I am the resurrection and the life," Jesus told her. "He who believes in me will live, even though he dies; and whoever lives and believes in me will never die. Do you believe this?" (John 11:25–26, NIV).

While Martha's "new" understanding of Jesus' true identity didn't answer all her questions, it did begin to prepare her for what Jesus was about to do on her behalf. And it also enabled her to bring her sister, Mary, to the One she needed to see that day above anyone else: Jesus Himself.

Martha told Jesus that she believed everything He had just told her, but she didn't just sit on that information. Instead, she took the action necessary to bring her sister to Him also: "And after she had said this, she went back and called her sister Mary aside. 'The Teacher is here,' she said, "and is asking for you'" (John 11:28, NIV).

I believe that Mary was literally emotionally unable to leave her home and go see Him. But Jesus did something He may very well do in our lives today when we're in such pain that we can't approach Him: He sent someone else, her sister, Martha, to let her know that He not only knew about her pain but also wanted to see her. Martha had received her word from God, and if she didn't understand much, she still had enough to pass along to her sister. In fact, it was the best and wisest thing she could have said to help her sister.

"Go to Jesus."

"SHE GOT UP QUICKLY…."

Mary received Martha's summons as good news. It's obvious from her response that she really wanted to see Him. "When Mary heard this, she got up quickly and went to him" (John 11:29, NIV).

Mary could easily have gone to Jesus before He sent for her through Martha. Instead she chose to stay home. I believe that is because deep down Mary really wanted to go to Jesus. She wanted to find out why He had allowed Lazarus to die, why He hadn't kept His word that her brother's sickness wouldn't end in death, and why He had allowed her to suffer the way she had.

Mary was like so many of us when we are hurting: While part of us wants to see the person we hold responsible for our pain, another part wants to avoid the situation altogether. Sometimes in a situation like that, all it takes to bring us to a point of seeing that person is knowing that they want to see us, that they want to be reconciled, and that they want to "clear the air."

When Mary heard that Jesus wanted to see her, she went to Him *quickly*. No foot dragging there! And she hurried because someone who loved her—and who loved Jesus—had given her a personal word telling her that He wanted to talk to her, even though He knew she was broken and perplexed.

Mary understood something that we all need to understand today: When we are hurting and in tears, Jesus wants to see us— even though we may have gone through a time when our pain kept us from approaching Him.

And He wants to see our tears for one reason: so that He may share in our pain and weeping with us.

Believe it, my friend, it's true!

OUR SAVIOR'S TEARS

When Mary finally saw Jesus up close and personal, she didn't greet Him in the way you might expect someone to greet the man she called her Lord and Teacher. She didn't give Him so much as an obligatory "Hello!" The very first words she said—between sobs and tears—as she fell at His feet were, "Lord, if you had been here, my brother would not have died!"

Again, there's the complaint.

When I imagine this scene in my mind's eye, I don't see a woman who approached Jesus with tears in her eyes and a lump in her throat. I see a storm of emotion! I see Mary fall at His feet, clutching the hem of His robe as if hanging on for dear life. I see

Mary pounding the ground—or maybe on Jesus Himself—her body racked with sobs.

This was four days' worth of searing pain, disappointment, frustration, and anger coming out all at once. This was absolutely raw emotion coming from a woman who had lost someone she loved deeply and dearly—even though she had been *promised* it wouldn't end like that. It was as if her mind and words were acknowledging who He was—"Lord"—but her tears and emotions were saying, "This is *Your* fault! I'm hurting and suffering a huge loss because You didn't keep Your word to me!"

How many of us have had one of those "if You had only been here" moments in our walk with Jesus? How many of us have looked at a really difficult situation in our lives and thought to ourselves, If only Jesus had shown up, I wouldn't be in this painful situation? I think it's safe to say that most of us have thought these very things, but were too afraid to put them into words, fearing that God might strike us dead on the spot.

But that's not what happened. Far from it!

Let's take another look at how Jesus responded to Mary's tears and anger. Did He pull her up to her feet and give her a good shake until she settled down? Did He just turn His back on her in disgust?

Not according to the Bible I read! Jesus looked beyond Mary's pain and anger and into her heart. But not only that, He actually entered into her pain with her. He heard her when she called Him "Lord" and shared with her in her pain. John tells us, "When Jesus saw her weeping, and the Jews who had come along with her weeping also, He was deeply moved in spirit and troubled" (John 11:33, NIV).

What we have here is a beautiful picture of worship during a time of sorrow and distress. We have a woman who knew and loved Jesus as her Lord but who couldn't understand why He hadn't come sooner. She just couldn't grasp why He hadn't shown mercy to their little family, touching her brother before it was too late. But not only that, we have a beautiful picture of a Savior who cared when she was hurting to the point of weeping Himself, emotionally moved by her tears.

But Jesus' response to this woman wasn't just an inner-emotional one. When He saw her emotion He was moved in spirit, and He allowed her and others to see how this scene had affected Him. John 11:35, the shortest verse in the Bible, says it all: "Jesus wept."

Earlier, I talked about the different reasons why Jesus was moved to tears, but there are some other things about this scene I don't want you to miss. First of all, Jesus wept with Mary because she had honestly and openly brought her tears and pain to Him. He was affected by her tears, very much like most of us would be when we see someone we care about in anguish.

Second, He wept only after she had left her house and come to Him to show Him her pain. This was not a Mary-to-Jesus time of prayer where everything was peaceful and pretty, with words of praise and adoration falling from her lips. It wasn't Mary worshiping

Jesus and telling Him how full of joy she was over His presence and His love. This was a time when the only way Mary could be honest with Jesus was to let Him hear and see how hurt and disappointed she was.

Mary let Him see her crying.

At that moment, of course, she couldn't see beyond the moment or beyond her own circumstances. If she had been able to see just a few minutes into the future, she would have come to Jesus shouting, smiling, and laughing because she would have known that her brother's story wasn't over at all. She would have known she was about to witness not just a nation-shaking miracle, but a miracle on her behalf.

Here's some good news for us today: Jesus is the same Jesus. He's the same yesterday and today. He's the same forever. And just as He stepped into the pain of Mary and Martha and took them far beyond their own expectations and hopes, He wants to step into our pain, too. He cares about our tears, just as He cared about Mary's tears.

Most believers have no problem believing in a God who rolls up His sleeves and moves into our lives to make us better Christians— better reflections of Jesus to a desperately needy world. But too many of us have a tough time believing that God cares and feels our pain with us. We're not sure where He is when we're hurting so bad that all we can do is cry out to Him. But the truth is, Jesus pays very close attention to our tears, and when we bring our sorrow to Him, He is profoundly affected and reaches out to share with us in our pain.

And He does those things today from a position of perfect understanding.

HE CARES, HE UNDERSTANDS

Could there be any better friend or loved one than the one who knows exactly what we need when we're in pain, disappointed, frustrated, or afraid? I'm talking about someone who can see and understand what we're facing and enduring—one who has the discernment to sense when we need a word of wisdom or encouragement and when we just need a listening ear or a shoulder to cry on.

I don't know about you, but I pray to have just that kind of friend when I'm in a time of need and pain. I also pray that I might *be* that kind of friend.

If you're a married man reading this book, you may have learned the importance of understanding that your wife's tears aren't always telling you that it's time to step in and fix what's wrong with her. Sometimes, her tears are just telling you to keep your mouth shut, put your arms around her, and share in her pain.

It's probably no great news flash that most men are "wired" to solve problems. When we recognize that our mates are in pain, we just naturally tend to want to fix things. That can be an excellent attribute when it comes time to repair the car or paint the house, but it can be a real hindrance when it comes to meeting with our wives in the midst of their pain.

Sometimes when our wives weep it's because they want us to take action. But I'd say that more often than not, our wives just want us to listen to them.

You've probably heard the old expression, "Too soon old, too late smart." Well, in this case, I'm glad I've finally come around. I've come to a point of better understanding my wife and what she needs from me.

The truth is, we humans—men and women, educated and uneducated alike—will always be limited in our understanding of one another. We won't always be able to grasp what others need from us when they're hurting. That's why so many of us (especially us men) will sometimes stumble when we try to meet the needs of someone with broken emotions.

We never have to worry about that with Jesus, though. He understands us intimately and perfectly, and He knows how each of us as individuals is "wired." He knows us infinitely better than any human can—better than we know ourselves. And because He knows us so perfectly, He always responds to our tears and our pain in just the right way.

Although Martha and Mary's words to Jesus when they first saw Him were identical, His responses to these two women were very different. I believe that's because He understood what each of them as individuals needed that day. Earlier, I showed you how Jesus gave Martha information. While it didn't solve her problem right away, it settled her heart to the point that she could run home and fetch her sister.

Mary, on the other hand, had a very different personality and emotional makeup. She couldn't have cared less about the information; she just wanted Jesus to know how her heart was hurting over what had happened.

In short, Martha operated on an informational level, while Mary operated on an emotional level. Martha needed teaching, while Mary just needed someone to cry with her.

There's the kind of grief we feel when we need answers, but there's also the kind of grief when all we long for is the listening ear and feeling heart of a friend. Sometimes when we are crying out to God in pain, we need Him to tell us why things have turned out the way they have and what He's going to do about it. But there are other times when we don't want an explanation and don't want information. We just want someone to step into our lives and feel our hurt with us.

The wonderful news is that we have a Savior who not only knows exactly what we need when we cry, but One who is more than able and more than willing to give it to us. Our part in this bargain is to simply allow God to see our tears and hear us cry.

We must come to Him.

ALLOWING JESUS TO SEE OUR TEARS

The Bible contains several examples of people allowing God to see their tears. The book of Psalms, a collection of 150 poems to God by various writers, expresses a wide array of emotions, including sadness and disappointment. Several of the psalms show us that shedding tears to God is not only acceptable to Him, but also beneficial. Here are some beautiful examples:

- I am weary with my sighing; every night I make my bed swim, I dissolve my couch with my tears. (Psalm 6:6)
- Hear my prayer, O LORD, and give ear to my cry; do not be silent at my tears; for I am a stranger with You, a sojourner like all my fathers. (Psalm 39:12)
- My tears have been my food day and night, while they say to me all day long, "Where is your God?" (Psalm 42:3)
  - You have taken account of my wanderings; put my tears in Your bottle; are they not in Your book? (Psalm 56:8)

The psalmists, who lived centuries before the arrival of Jesus Christ, knew that they could allow God to know about their pain, to hear their crying, and to see their tears. They weren't trying to manipulate Him or force a certain response, they were honestly and openly expressing what was in their hearts.

We should never hide our tears or sorrow from Jesus. He is our

Lord and Savior, but He is also the Best Friend we will ever have. And when we are honest with Him about our feelings and allow Him to see our brokenness and our tears, we can do so knowing that He loves us and notes every single tear.

Near the very end of the Bible, we read this magnificent promise: "He [Jesus] will wipe every tear from their eyes. There will be no more death or mourning or crying or pain, for the old order of things has passed away" (Revelation 21:4, NIV).

What a promise! There is a day coming when there will be no more tears of pain and mourning, only the tears of joy we may shed as we begin eternity in the presence of our loving heavenly Father. But in the meantime, we can be assured that God cares when we cry, that He is willing and able to share with us in our tears and in our pain, and that He wants to give us comfort.

Our Lord cares when we're hurting so bad and crying so hard that we feel incapable of taking our pain to Him. As the psalmist wrote, "For his anger endureth but a moment; in his favour is life: weeping may endure for a night, but joy cometh in the morning" (Psalm 30:5, KJV).

Jesus saw Mary's tears and the tears of those who mourned with her, and He was touched and moved to tears Himself. And when we allow Him to see our tears today—sincere tears that come from the pain of a broken heart over what we've lost—we can know that He'll enter into our pain, comfort us, dry our tears, and turn our sorrow into joy.

So don't stay home when the tears come. Don't close your heart. Don't try to "go it alone," believing that Jesus doesn't care. Get in His presence and pour out your heart before Him. He not only understands, He cares more deeply than you can imagine.

7

God, Do You Really Care...
WHEN I QUESTION YOU?

For a number of years now, the National Football League has employed a high-tech system called "instant replay," designed to help correct and possibly overrule the errors of game officials. According to the instant replay rule, the head coach of a team throws a red flag on the field when he thinks one of the officials missed a call—such as awarding a touchdown that shouldn't have been a touchdown or incorrectly ruling a receiver out of bounds on a pass play.

When the referee sees the red flag, he knows it's time to go to the coach to find out what the challenge is about. From there, he heads to the replay booth to review the call. Sometimes the call is reversed, but sometimes the referee rules that the play was too close to reverse—or that the covering official got it right the first time. In that case, the call stands and the team who challenged the ruling is charged with a timeout.

Some believers remind me of that football coach with the red flag. God makes a call in their lives, and they think He's gotten it wrong. They think He ought to review, reconsider, and even reverse the call.

In short, they believe God has "blown it," and ought to make things right.

I don't think there is a believer who has ever lived who hasn't at some point in his or her walk with Jesus questioned God and plainly asked Him, *Why me? Why now? Why this?* When we do that, what we're really asking Him is whether He knows our situations, knows what He's doing in the midst of them, and really knows what's best for us.

The devil loves that. He loves to see any sort of erosion in your confidence toward God. He'd like you to believe that God doesn't know what He's doing in your life, that He's making a mistake when He asks you to do something, and that He doesn't really have a reasonable plan for you. Bottom line, Satan would love to have you believe that God is in just a little bit over His head. And if the evil one can get you to buy into that kind of thinking, then he can lure you into "helping" God along with His plan for you—or even coming up with a more "reasonable and logical" plan of your own.

Does God care about that?

Does God care when we question His wisdom, question His attentiveness, question His love?

I want to address that by looking at some interaction between Jesus and Martha as He was about to raise her brother Lazarus from the dead.

TIME FOR A MIRACLE—BUT FIRST...

Jesus was about to perform the very miracle that the events recorded in John 11 had been leading up to, and as He approached Lazarus's stone-sealed tomb, He gave a very simple instruction: "Remove the stone."

We'd like to think that Martha would have just kept quiet and watched Jesus at work once the stone was removed. After all, just a few moments earlier she had acknowledged, "Even now I know that whatever You ask of God, God will give You" (John 11:22).

Great words of confidence! But seconds later, when she heard Jesus' command to open up her brother's tomb, she threw the red flag. She wanted a review of that decision, pointing out what she knew to be a certainty, given the fact that Lazarus had been dead for so long: "Lord, by this time there will be a stench; for he has been dead four days" (John 11:39).

Martha was doing more than pointing out the obvious. Of course Jesus knew that a body lying in a grave for four full days would have the overpowering stink of death on it. In reality, what she was doing was questioning Jesus' instructions. What she was asking Him in reality was, "Why would You make such a request?" In her natural mind—one that still didn't fully comprehend what Jesus was about to do—opening that grave made no earthly sense.

Martha was far from the first person in the Bible to openly question God's instructions. For example, when the Lord first appeared to Moses and told him that he had been chosen to lead the people of Israel out of Egyptian bondage and slavery, all Moses could do was tell Him how unqualified he was to carry out such an awesome task. Moses was sure that God was making a big mistake sending someone like him, a man who couldn't speak and couldn't lead (or so he thought).

We see another example in Judges 6. The angel of the Lord approached a young man named Gideon, who was threshing grain in a winepress out of fear of marauding bands of Midianites. "The LORD is with you, O valiant warrior" (6:12).

Gideon didn't feel anything like a warrior—let alone a valiant one.

He challenged his divine visitor. "O my lord, if the LORD is with us, when then has all this happened to us? And where are all His miracles which our fathers told us about? ...Now the LORD has abandoned us and given us into the hand of Midian" (6:13).

Undeterred by Gideon's weak response, the angel of the Lord

commissioned him: "Go in this your strength and deliver Israel from the hand of Midian. Have I not sent you?" (6:14).

Gideon still wasn't convinced, and again questioned the Lord's judgment.

"O Lord, how shall I deliver Israel? Behold, my family is the least in Manasseh, and I am the youngest in my father's house" (6:15).

Patiently, the Lord came back with strong instructions—and a strong promise. "Surely I will be with you, and you shall defeat Midian as one man" (6:16).

Both of these biblical scenes remind us that God doesn't always do things the way we think He should. They also show us that it is entirely possible to love God, to call Him "Lord" from the heart, but also question Him. But most of all, they are reminders that when He asks us to do something—even when it seems strange to us—we are to obey. It is only in our full obedience that we will receive His blessings.

THE STRUGGLE TO BELIEVE

To this day—perhaps now more than ever—people struggle when it comes to believing what God has said and doing what He has told them to do. Many of us, it seems, question Him, wanting to know "what's in it for us" if we take the step and obey Him. This is especially true when it comes to those things that seem unreasonable to us, or "outside the box."

But John's account of the scene at Lazarus's grave shows us that it's the *tone* of the questioning that makes a difference to God.

Martha wasn't the only one at this scene questioning Jesus—nor the only one who wondered if He knew what He was doing. Earlier, I pointed out that some of the Jews who had come from Jerusalem to Bethany to comfort Mary and Martha—including some, no doubt, who opposed Jesus—had a question of their own: "Could not this man, who opened the eyes of the blind man, have kept this man also from dying?" (John 11:37).

There's a big difference in tone between the questioning of the unbelievers and that of Martha. On the one hand, there were already deep doubts—and cynicism so thick you could cut it with a knife. The Jews who had come to comfort the family weren't simply questioning Jesus, they were questioning His credentials as Messiah.

Martha, on the other hand, loved Jesus with all of her heart. And it was she who had earlier recognized Him as One who received from the Father's hand everything He asked for. While the unbelievers at the gravesite called Jesus "this man," Martha called Him "Lord."

Martha's perplexity was mixed with faith. Her questions and heartbreak were shot through with love. And He was about to lead her into a deeper understanding of His nature and purpose.

To those who questioned Him and utterly dismissed His power over sickness and death, however, Jesus had nothing to say at all.

THINKING IN THE MIRACULOUS

We all know how the Lazarus story ended: with the greatest miracle Martha or Mary or anyone else at the scene had ever seen. Before the miracle actually took place, however, Martha had no idea how the story would play out. Her mind, already locked up with grief and sorrow, simply could not process the turn of events. Jesus had not come when she and Mary called. But He had sent a message clearly stating that Lazarus's illness would not end in death. And then Lazarus died! And then Jesus arrived on the scene and told her that He was the resurrection and the light.

Nothing made sense.

Everything seemed in turmoil.

She still had no clue what He had in mind for her and for Lazarus.

Even so, in spite of everything, in the face of all those questions-without-answers, she acknowledged Jesus as Lord.

Then came that strange, disturbing command to remove the stone from the mouth of the tomb—and all she could think about was how bad the body was going to smell after four days.

Because we know in hindsight what Jesus was about to do, it

might be easy for some of us to criticize Martha. After all, this was *Jesus* she was talking to, not just some man on the street. Of course she should have expected a miracle and of course she should have obeyed His command without questioning Him.

And Moses should have obeyed the Lord without questioning Him.

And Gideon should have obeyed the Lord without questioning Him.

But they did question Him…and in His grace and power He used them anyway.

I believe we need to cut Martha some slack here. First of all, if you've ever suffered deep grief, you'll know that it's hard to even think straight at times. In truth, she was doing exactly what most of us would have done in that situation: responding to the natural facts as she knew them.

Jesus knew what was behind Martha's questions, but He was about to move her from the natural—from the facts of the world as she saw them—to a more spiritual level of thinking. He wanted her to catch a glimpse of the wonderful, miraculous plan He had for her life.

GOD'S PLAN, STEP BY STEP

We need to notice that Jesus had told Martha what He wanted her to do before He revealed what He would do. He didn't tell her,

"Remove the stone and I will raise Lazarus from the dead." He simply said, "Remove the stone," a command that required a response from Martha.

But why didn't Jesus just tell Martha His whole plan when He gave the command for the stone to be moved? Because He was in the process of bringing her to a point of acting on what He had already told her, so that she could receive the blessing He had for her. This was a miracle-in-waiting, but it wasn't going to happen until the stone was moved.

Most of us want to know the details of what God is doing before we obey Him, don't we? We want just a little peek at His future plans for us before we sign on the dotted line. We want to know when we'll get that better job, when we'll find a mate, when things will change for us, when God will meet a particular need in our lives. That is why we tend to question God when He instructs us to do something that seems strange or even unreasonable.

Earlier, I pointed out that God doesn't give us all the particulars of His plans for us. In fact, sometimes He doesn't tell us His plan at all. Sometimes He keeps some things secret from us until the time and situation are right.

And that might not be until eternity. Can we handle that?

In the Old Testament, it's described this way: "The secret things belong to the Lord our God, but the things revealed belong to us and to our sons forever, that we may observe all the words of this law" (Deuteronomy 29:29).

In other words, while God sometimes reveals certain things to us, there are many other things He keeps secret and does not unveil for us until the time, the situation, and our hearts are right. It's important to understand that part of His character, and it's also important to know that oftentimes God won't reveal His *secret* will to us until we have been obedient to His *revealed* will.

Allow me to illustrate.

Let's say I was planning to build a house. I've never built a house before, but I have all the detailed instructions starting with the excavation of the plot my house will sit on and ending with the interior decorating. These plans, however, are unique in that I can only read them one step at a time. I can't move on to the next step until I have finished the one before it. No peeking at Step *D* until I've completed Steps *A, B,* and *C.*

Well, I'm really impatient, and I want to know how the house will shape up, and just what it is I'm building on every day. I want to know what it will look like when it's *done.* I want to know the styles, the dimensions, the features, the colors. But I know I can't have the answers I crave until I follow the steps leading up to the actual finishing of the house. And it all starts with what I know comes first: bulldozing the lot where the house will be built. Only after I have done that can I move on to building the foundation, framing, sheetrocking, and all the other steps required to finish my house.

God often works in our lives in much the same way. He reveals to us only what we need to know to take us to a particular point in His plan for us, and only after we've taken that first step will He tell us what we need to know to get to the next step. In other words, when God has a plan to take us from point A to point C in our lives, He's not going to show us what point C is until we've obediently gone with Him to point B. If we aren't willing to go to point B—no matter how strange or confusing it may seem or no matter how it doesn't appear to fit into the plan of making it to point C—then God won't show us how He wants us to get to point C.

Sadly, many believers have that backwards. They have their own stones that must be moved from their own graves before God will reveal to them His miracle-in-the-making. But they want to know the *whole* plan before they're willing to move those personal stones.

And why are we so often reluctant to move the stones God has told us to move? Simply because there are many times when His requests seem so strange to us.

STRANGE COMMANDS

I don't want you to take this wrong, but in our human understanding God's logic can seem pretty weird sometimes. That's nothing new either, because the Bible is filled with examples of God commanding people to do some very strange things.

Why, in Joshua 3, have the Jewish priests dip their feet in the floodwaters of the Jordan River so that the people of Israel could cross? Why not just split the waters the way He did when Moses stretched out his rod over the Red Sea? Or better yet, why not supply everyone with boats?

Why, in Joshua 6, have the soldiers of Israel walk around the walls of Jericho quietly for six days, then have the priests blow their horns, when what they were looking for was a military victory? Why not just bless the troops with the supernatural ability to defeat the city militarily? Or easier still—why not just send fire and brimstone to take the city down and be done with it?

Why, in 2 Kings 5:10–14, have Naaman, the distinguished Syrian general, dip himself in the Jordan River seven times in order to heal him of leprosy? Why not just take it away miraculously by having someone lay hands on him?

Why, in John 9, give a blind man sight by smearing dirt and saliva in his eyes, then having him wash his face? Why not just heal him with a touch and a word and let him go on his way?

All of these incidents show us a God who sometimes does things in very strange and mysterious ways, ways that must have made the people involved wonder if He knew what He was doing (Naaman himself at first refused to do as the prophet Elisha had said because it seemed so foolish, but when he did…he was healed). In each instance, He gave people very specific instructions that just didn't seem to fit in with what He was trying to accomplish.

But God has His reasons for doing things and commanding His

people to do things that seem unreasonable or even a little crazy. In the examples above, God gave very specific—and seemingly bizarre—instructions, and required exact obedience to the very letter. And why? *Because He wanted to show His people that they had nothing to lose and everything to gain by following His instructions, even those that might have seemed "off" to them.*

We need to remember that our heavenly Father is infinite in His wisdom and in His personal knowledge of each of His children. He knows precisely what it takes to test, deepen, and refine our faith. More often than not, our faith grows best against the backdrop of things we don't fully understand, and not in the context of the things we do.

DID I NOT SAY TO YOU...?

When Martha pointed out that there would be a terrible stench coming from Lazarus's tomb if the stone was removed, Jesus almost seemed impatient. Again, instead of telling her what He was going to do, He told her, "Did I not say to you that if you believe, you will see the glory of God?"

Let's focus on how Jesus began this reminder: "Did not I say to you…" As Jesus gave Martha what sounded like a mild rebuke, He did so by bringing her attention back to what He had already said, by reminding her that He had promised that Lazarus's illness wouldn't end in death and that he would rise again.

At that point in this story, Martha was in a very difficult place. She had taken her eyes off of Jesus' earlier promises and had focused instead on her present situation. In that moment, she was focused on death, not on Jesus. And how had she come to that point? She had left God's word.

When we take our eyes off God and His word, we have nothing to look to but situations, speculations, and human reasoning. When we turn away from God's instructions and commands, we find ourselves following the footsteps of the prophet Jonah, before he was disciplined and corrected by the Lord.

And nobody wants to attend *that* school.

YOU'RE SENDING ME *WHERE?*

Jonah had received from God what he considered a very strange command: "Arise, go to Nineveh the great city and cry against it, for their wickedness has come up before Me" (Jonah 1:2).

Nineveh?

What in the world was God thinking? The huge capital of the Assyrian Empire, Nineveh, was Israel's bitter and brutal enemy. *You've got to be kidding me, Lord,* Jonah must have been thinking. *Why would You waste my time and Yours sending me to preach to such a bunch of bloodthirsty heathens?*

In Jonah's mind, it would have made more sense if God had commanded him to tell his own people that Nineveh was about to be destroyed. To him, going to preach to a bunch of Assyrians must have seemed like giving aid and comfort to Israel's worst enemy. So rather than obey the voice of the Lord, Jonah followed his own logic, and fled from His presence.

And it was all downhill from there.

The Bible says that Jonah went down to a place called Joppa, where he boarded a ship and fled for Tarshish, about two thousand miles from Israel. But as God will do when He gives us a personal word, He tracked this wayward prophet every step of the way.

As Jonah's ship made its way across the Mediterranean, the Lord sent a storm so violent that even the experienced seamen on board feared for their lives. The situation looked so grim that the ship's captain—himself a non-believer—called on Jonah to pray to God that they might survive the storm. Though the men on board weren't believers, they began asking who could have angered God so much that He would send such a ferocious storm. Finally, Jonah fessed up and told them that he was a Hebrew, running from the Almighty. "Throw me overboard," he told them, "and that will take care of the storm."

Jonah had come to a point where he believed he was better off dead, but God wasn't finished with him yet. So instead of allowing him to drown, He sent a great fish to swallow the runaway prophet whole.

Because Jonah had not only questioned God but also refused to do what He had commanded him, he got to spend some time thinking and praying...in the stomach of the fish, a place so foul and putrid that it defied imagination.

Jonah spent three days and nights in the fish's belly, and when he finally got his head and his heart right with God, the fish vomited him up on dry land, where God was waiting for him.

And what was the first thing God said? "Arise, go to Nineveh the great city" (Jonah 3:2). It still must have sounded crazy to Jonah. It still didn't make any sense to him. But this time, he didn't argue or run. He simply obeyed.

After a three-day journey, he began his preaching campaign in the enemy capital...where the people turned to God in droves.

The Book of Jonah demonstrates that God's word to and for us isn't going to change just because we question Him—or even run from Him. As I write these words, I could tell you about believers who are logging their own time in fish bellies—or places just as bad. Why? Because they can't grasp the fact that if anyone's going to change, it's got to be them, not God. God will never change—either His character, His mind, His promises, or His commands.

When we realize that He may sometimes ask us to do what seems to us strange or weird simply for the purpose of teaching us to trust Him, we will find peace—peace within ourselves and peace with Him. And not only will we have peace, we will be in a position to see God do something miraculous in our lives.

Maybe even a resurrection.

BELIEVING BEFORE SEEING

God wants us to understand a simple but profound principle of faith: believing comes before seeing. We must believe what He tells us before we can see what He intends to do.

Time after time in the Bible, we see examples of people believing God then seeing Him fulfill great promises on their behalf. Abraham didn't get to enjoy the promised blessings from God until he believed in his heart. Moses didn't get to take such a high place in Jewish history until he believed God would fulfill His every promise. And the people of Israel didn't get to see the Promised Land until they learned to trust and believe the same God who had miraculously delivered their forefathers from Egyptian captivity.

So many of us have that backwards, don't we? We live by the old saying "Seeing is believing," and want God to show us something before we believe Him and follow His specific directions.

That is exactly why Jesus asked Martha the "did I not tell you" question the way He did. He was essentially saying to her, "You don't need to tell Me that the body will smell bad. I'm well aware that your brother has been dead for four days. But that doesn't matter to Me because I'm about to do something to change all that. So if you're done questioning Me now, do as I asked you and move the stone."

Although we don't like to admit it, many of us question God simply because we don't really believe Him! And that's sad...because until we believe God, we can't expect to receive anything from Him. As the apostle James wrote, "But he must ask in faith without any doubting, for the one who doubts is like the surf of the sea, driven and tossed by the wind. For that man ought not to expect that he will receive anything from the Lord, being a double-minded man, unstable in all his ways" (James 1:6–8).

We need to understand that our God doesn't waste words and He doesn't say something without having a reason for it or without expecting us to respond. When Jesus said, "Move the stone," He wasn't just speaking to hear Himself talk. There was a reason for those words, and it was to encourage Martha—and the others at the scene, including the disciples—toward a deeper faith and trust in Him, as well as a willingness to obey.

Let's face it, sometimes we're more interested in asking God questions than we are in simply hearing and obeying what He's already told us. Because of that, I believe, we miss His best for our lives.

There's nothing necessarily wrong with asking God questions. The patriarchs did it. So did the prophets and the psalmists. Ditto with the Gospels...beginning with Mary's question for the angel Gabriel after he had told her she would conceive and give birth to the Christ: "How can this be, since I am a virgin?" (Luke 1:34).

This was an example of someone who believed God but who wanted to know how He was going to do what He had said. In other words, it was a question of the mechanics of the process. In the end, after Gabriel told Mary how she would become pregnant, she voiced what had been in her heart all along: "Behold, the bondslave of the Lord; may it be done to me according to your word" (Luke 1:38).

Mary believed the angel when he said, "Nothing is impossible with God." She had questions, but more importantly she believed God could do as He had said. Far too many believers, however, run into problems when they allow their questions about what God is doing to paralyze them—and keep them from fully believing Him and acting on their faith.

When Jesus said, "Remove the stone," Martha had a decision to make, and it's the same one so many of us are faced with today. Will we focus on our questions about what God asks us to do, then allow those questions to become unbelief? Or will we commit ourselves to doing as God tells us to do, no matter what?

Martha would vote for the latter option.

Obeying a puzzling command led to the happiest day in her life.

--- 8 ---

God, Do You Really Care...

WHEN I DON'T
BELIEVE?

Most of us have the faith-thing down when it comes to the basics.

We believe that Jesus is the one and only Son of God.

We believe He came to earth to die for our sins, so that we can live forever.

We even believe that God's Holy Spirit empowers us to live as He wants us to live and do the things He wants us as His children to do.

But there's a question some of us just aren't ready to tackle yet.

We have trouble believing that God truly loves us and is working for our good when we are crushed by tragedy, pain, heartbreak, and loss. When our world collapses around us and we lose something we hold near and dear, we have a hard time believing that God is really involved, or that God really cares.

Does that matter to God? What do you think?

Does God notice and care when we don't believe?

I'd say that He cares about that more than anything. Why? Because our whole relationship with Him is based on faith—our ability and willingness to believe Him and take Him at His word. And when we come to a place in our lives when our faith unravels into unbelief, He will do whatever it takes to restore that faith, and bring us to a point of believing everything He has told us through His written Word, the Bible.

That is exactly what He did with His dear friends Mary and Martha, women who believed in and loved Jesus, but who somehow hadn't retained what He had already promised them.

LET ME SAY IT AGAIN...

Earlier I pointed out how Jesus prepared the people at Lazarus's gravesite for a miracle when He made what seemed to be a very strange command: "Remove the stone." Martha responded to this command with what seemed to be a logical—and obvious—observation: "Lord, by this time there will be a stench; for he has been dead four days."

But now I want to focus on what Jesus replied to Martha in that moment—and what it meant to her...and to us. When Martha made that comment about the stench, Jesus came back with a reply that sounded almost aggravated: "Did I not say to you that if you believe, you will see the glory of God?" (John 11:40).

But if He sounded a little impatient with Martha, it was because He wanted to drive home a point, and it's this: He had given her a promise, and it was a promise He fully intended to keep...if she would only believe Him.

There is a very real connection between this statement and one Jesus made to His men before they left Perea to travel to Bethany. After telling a confused and frightened bunch of disciples that they would be going with Him to Bethany so they could awaken Lazarus from his sleep, Jesus finally got down to the meat and potatoes of His mission: "Lazarus is dead, and I am glad for your sakes that I was not there, *so that you may believe*" (John 11:14–15).

Everything Jesus did and said in this account was for one purpose, and that was that those who heard His words and saw His deeds would believe. He delayed coming to Lazarus's side so that people would see the glory of God through his illness...and believe. He waited and was glad He did so simply so that the disciples would see what was about to happen...and believe. And He took the time to talk to Martha so that she would hear His words and see His works...and believe.

He does the very same thing for us today.

And belief is still a very, very important issue to Him.

I am firmly convinced that God allows, or even causes, a lot of the trials and difficulties we go through today—illnesses, loss, various deaths, and other things—so that our faith will be established, tested, or strengthened.

Nothing is more important to God than having His children believe Him and His every word. God relates to each and every one of us on the basis of faith. So when we as believers come a point where life doesn't make sense, when we are going through a crisis that seems to have no meaning, when God seems completely absent in our situations, it may very well be that He is putting us in a place where we will learn to believe Him without reservation.

WHAT IT *REALLY* MEANS TO BELIEVE

We've all heard sayings that go something like this: "God won't put you through more than you can bear."

There's a grain of truth to that. God can and will give us the strength to endure anything. But I think the premise of it is a little backwards. Sometimes life's situations—the very ones God puts us in—can become literally unbearable.

But He has a reason for that, too. When God delays stepping into our life situations, when it seems He's put us in or allowed us to step into situations that we can't humanly bear, it's because He's up to something bigger, something of eternal value. And not only that, He is *glad* to do so because in the long run it stretches us and strengthens us and deepens our faith.

In order to get a grip on this aspect of God's nature, we need to understand what it means to believe or to have faith. The writer of the book of Hebrews defines faith as "the substance of things hoped for, the evidence of things not seen. For by it the elders obtained a good testimony. By faith we understand that the worlds were framed by the word of God, so that the things which are seen were not made of things which are visible" (Hebrews 11:1–3, NKJV).

Faith, then, isn't a matter of what we can see, hear, smell, or touch. It's having the conviction or the assurance of something for which there is no empirical or physical support or proof. It's being absolutely convinced of some fact or truth, even though neither your physical senses nor human reasoning can grasp it, see it, smell it, or touch it.

The Bible very regularly makes the distinction between that which we know by sight and that which we know by faith. When you see something (or perceive it with any of your physical senses) you know it's there simply because the visual evidence tells you so. In other words, it's right before your eyes. But when you have faith in something God has told you or shown you, you can't always see it. Even so, you are convinced of its truth because you perceive it on a spiritual level.

BLIND FAITH?

We've all heard the term "blind faith." In the world's eyes, that means that we believe in something even though there is no evidence at all for it, physical or otherwise. Although our faith is oftentimes rooted in what we can't see, that doesn't mean there is no evidence or substance behind it. In fact, completely the opposite is true.

The writer of Hebrews tells us that faith is, "the substance of things hoped for." In other words, for faith to have meaning there must be something of substance behind it, even if it can't be proved with physical evidence. We don't put faith in the Tooth Fairy, Santa Claus, or the Easter Bunny because we know that they don't really exist and that there is no substance behind them. On the other hand, we believe in God and believe His Word because He has identified Himself in a historical and spiritual book called the Bible.

Hebrews tells us the importance of that kind of faith later in chapter 11: "And without faith it is impossible to please Him, for he who comes to God must believe that He is, and that He is a rewarder of those who seek Him" (Hebrews 11:6).

That was exactly what Jesus was talking to Martha about when He said, "Did I not say to you, if you believe you will see the glory of God?" Jesus wanted Martha to understand with her heart and see with her spiritual eyes that He was real and that He was everything she had believed He was. He also wanted her to understand that *because* of who He was, she could believe and trust Him to keep His word to her.

IN GOD WE (REALLY CAN) TRUST

Most of us have met people—or perhaps know them well—who are, in politically correct terms, "truth challenged."

In plain, unvarnished English, they're liars.

We can't believe anything they say, even when they are telling the truth, because we know their character and know they are prone to being untruthful.

God's character is exactly the opposite of that in every way. We can believe everything He says, simply because it is not in His character to lie or to renege on a promise. He is the very embodiment of the word *trustworthy*, so we can count on Him completely.

In his historic "I Have a Dream" speech, Martin Luther King said, "I have a dream that my four little children will one day live in a nation where they will not be judged by the color of their skin but by the content of their character."

That dream is as important today as it was when Dr. King declared it years ago. It's foolish to make a decision about a person's character on the basis of skin color or any other external feature. We have to know what's inside a person before we can draw any conclusions about the content of his or her character and trustworthiness. The same is true when it comes to our relationship with God. When we look at the content of His character, we can know that it's safe to take His every word to the bank.

One thing God really loves is when we hold up His promises before Him and hold Him to His own word. That's because He loves showing His people that He is a God who is true to Himself, and therefore true to His own words. To God, this is not an "I dare you" challenge but a demonstration that we believe Him.

The apostle Paul pointed this out in his letter to the Roman church: "What if some did not have faith? Will their lack of faith nullify God's faithfulness? Not at all! Let God be true, and every man a liar. As it is written: 'So that you may be proved right when you speak and prevail when you judge'" (Romans 3:3–4, NIV).

One of God's promises believers throughout the ages have been watching for expectantly is the return of Jesus for His church. Jesus promised the disciples that He would return, but He didn't—and couldn't—tell them exactly when that would happen: "But of that day and hour no one knows, not even the angels of heaven, nor the Son, but the Father alone" (Matthew 24:36).

But while Jesus couldn't say exactly when He would return, He did point the disciples toward signs of that event, things we now call the "signs of the times." A sign is something that doesn't point toward itself but toward something else. The Bible—including many of the words of Jesus Himself—gives us many signs of Jesus' imminent return.

There has been a lot of debate within the church through the centuries over exactly what Jesus meant when He talked about the signs of His return. Are they literal, or do they point figuratively to other things?

While opinions on that subject vary widely, we can be sure of one thing: We will see signs that His return is near. That is what Jesus was talking about when He told the disciples, "Now learn the parable from the fig tree: when its branch has already become tender, and put forth its leaves, you know that summer is near; so, you too, when you see all these things, recognize that He is near, right at the door" (Matthew 24:32–33).

PAY CLOSE ATTENTION

We need to not only listen to what God has said about our Lord's return, but also pay close attention to what He is doing in the world around us. In other words, we need to link the promises of the Word with the signs of the times.

Many believers have a difficult time doing that. They know what the Lord has *said* to them, but they don't seem to be able to make the connection between His words and what He's actually up to in their very own lives—especially when they're hurting or confused.

This is where Martha fell short.

Jesus gave a command to open up her brother's tomb, and all she could think about was how bad death would smell. Instead of making a connection between what He had already said—both in His message from Perea and when He first spoke to her upon His arrival in Bethany—and what He was about to do, she focused on the bare facts of the situation. *Lazarus was dead. Dead bodies decay. Rolling the stone away would be offensive.*

When Jesus prodded Martha by asking her, "Did I not say to you...?" He was challenging her to pay closer attention to His word, to recall what He had already told her. That's the same challenge God gives us today, particularly in those times when we're hurting and life doesn't make much sense.

BELIEVING MEANS TAKING ACTION

Jesus told Martha that if she believed, she would see "the glory of God." But what did that mean?

It meant that she was going to see God being God.

It meant that Jesus' absolute power over death would be put on display for her and everyone at the scene to see for themselves.

But there was a simple condition to this promise: She had to believe, and she had to demonstrate that belief by standing by Lazarus's grave as the stone was removed.

When we believe God, we take action based on what we

know—that His word is truth. It's not based on what we can physically see, hear, and touch, and it's not based on what we can emotionally feel. There will be times in the life of every believer when feelings contradict what God is saying, when our emotions—as well as our rational minds—tell us that He's not really in control, that He's not really involved in our present situation, that He doesn't really care when we are sick, hurting, confused, or lacking the faith it takes to believe He will do what He's promised.

WHEN FAITH AND UNBELIEF COLLIDE

As strange as it may sound, faith and unbelief can exist at the very same time in the very same heart and mind. There is an example of this in the Gospel of Mark, which records an incident where Jesus is about to cast a particularly nasty demon out of the son of a man who approaches Him for help.

Jesus had just returned with Peter, James, and John from a scene we call the Transfiguration, up on a mountaintop. As Jesus and the three reached the foot of the mountain, they found that a commotion had broken out, because the disciples who had stayed behind had been asked to cast out the demon but couldn't. Out of the crowd came the afflicted boy's dad, pleading with Jesus to heal his son.

Jesus told the man to bring the boy to Him, and the second the spirit saw Jesus it threw the boy to the ground and sent him into convulsions. The father told Jesus that his son had been in that condition since he was a small child, and that the demon had several times thrown him into fires and into water trying to kill him. "If you can do anything, take pity on us and help us," the man begged.

Jesus, of course, was more than able to do whatever it took for this man's son to be made whole. As He did so often, He took the occasion of a miracle healing to teach an important spiritual truth. He wanted this distraught father to understand that anything could happen for him...if he only believed: "'If You can?' All things are possible to him who believes," Jesus told him. (Mark 9:23).

The man responded with something that was between a declaration of belief and a humble cry for help. At first glance, his response seems contradictory. "I do believe; help my unbelief" (Mark 9:24).

This is an example of a man who had enough faith to be honest with God about his unbelief. And it's also an example of a man who put action behind the faith he had by simply approaching Jesus and asking Him to heal his son. Jesus responded to this man's faith by first teaching him, then healing his son on the spot.

Here is something that *didn't* happen in Jesus' conversation with Martha at the tomb. Jesus reminded Martha of what He had just told her—that she would see the glory of God if she only believed. But as they stood in front of that tomb, Jesus did not turn to her and say, "*Now*, do you believe? Because if you can't tell me without hesitation that you believe, then we're done here." Jesus didn't verbally address Martha's doubts, other than to remind her of the importance of believing Him.

Instead, He just waited until the stone was moved…and life stepped out of death.

When Martha and Mary and the mourners who had come to comfort them stood before Lazarus's grave and heard Jesus tell them, "Remove the stone," they had been given a tangible way to demonstrate that they believed Him. I don't believe that was by accident, because I know that the same Jesus who can raise a man dead four days in the tomb could very easily have removed the stone without anyone's help.

Jesus' command to have the people there remove the stone had nothing to do with His need for it to be moved. He could have had Lazarus walk right through it—as He would do at His own resurrection. But He was simply giving them an opportunity to put action behind what they believed—even though they had questions about the wisdom of that action.

We've all heard the old saying, "You talk the talk, but do you walk the walk?" We can apply that to how we demonstrate that we believe God, because it's not just our words that demonstrate that we believe Him, but also our actions. The apostle James pointed that out when he wrote, "What use is it, my brethren, if a man says he has faith, but he has no works?" (James 2:14).

Many Christians never have the opportunity to see God moving in their lives in the way they want or need, simply because they don't demonstrate that they believe Him through their actions. They *talk* a good game of believing God, but when it comes right down to it, they aren't doing anything to show that they truly believe.

That is exactly the problem Jesus is addressing when He asks Martha, "Did I not say to you, if you believe, you will see the glory of God?" Jesus fully intended to do an awesome miracle on behalf of that little family in Bethany. But that was contingent on two things: believing Him and validating that belief by taking action.

ONE LAST STEP BEFORE A MIRACLE

With the stone out of the way, Jesus was ready to perform one of His best-known and most spectacular miracles. And as He made His final preparation to bring Lazarus out of the grave, He did what He so often did in key situations in His ministry.

He prayed.

John records the scene like this: "And Jesus lifted up His eyes and said, "Father, I thank You that You have heard Me. And I know that You always hear Me, but because of the people who are standing by I said this, that they may believe that You sent Me" (John 11:41–42, NKJV).

Jesus knew who He was.

He knew He was the Chosen One, the Son of God sent into the world to be our Savior. And He knew that He had the Father's ear and that He would receive anything He asked for. But we need to notice that Jesus didn't talk to the Father about what was about to happen until the people demonstrated that they believed Him by removing the stone from the grave.

The Bible tells us that Jesus not only justifies us before God but also pleads with the Father on our behalf: "Who will bring a charge against God's elect? God is the one who justifies; who is the one who condemns? Christ Jesus is He who died, yes, rather who was raised, who is at the right hand of God, who also intercedes for us" (Romans 8:33–34).

In the Bible, the word *intercession* means to "stand in the gap" on someone else's behalf. A good illustration of this is the work of a defense attorney—or as some defendants might call him, "a mouthpiece"—who stands in the gap between a judge and jury on behalf of a client in a criminal court case. Because a defendant has an attorney pleading his case, he doesn't need to worry over whether his side of the story is being heard.

That is what Jesus does for all of us. We need to understand that without Him, the only answer we will ever receive from the Father is no, simply because we are guilty, lost in our sins, and without access to Him. But because Jesus is at His right hand taking our requests to the Father, we can know that He hears and responds and gives the Son what He asks for on our behalf.

When we are walking through difficult times, it's easy to spend a lot of time talking to others, debating with ourselves over what we want to do, and dwelling on our pain and confusion. But these are the last things we need to be doing during those times! The first thing we should do when we are hurting is take our problems to our Intercessor, Jesus Christ. As we kneel before Him with hearts and minds of faith, He willingly steps into the gap between us and the Father.

That was the point of what Jesus was saying when He told the disciples, "If you abide in Me, and My words abide in you, ask whatever you wish, and it will be done for you" (John 15:7).

THE "SPECIFICS" OF A MIRACLE

Jesus wasn't raising the dead in general that day.

If He had simply said, "Come forth!" instead of "Lazarus, come forth!" He might have emptied every tomb in the world.

Worldwide resurrection, however, is an event yet to happen. The apostle Paul wrote about that wondrous moment yet to be: "For the Lord Himself will descend from heaven with a shout, with the voice of the archangel and with the trumpet of God, and the dead in Christ will rise first. Then we who are alive and remain will be caught up together with them in the clouds to meet the Lord in the air, and so we shall always be with the Lord" (1 Thessalonians 4:16–17).

Jesus was about to raise one man specifically—a man whose sisters and friends had shown just enough faith to believe that He would do something miraculous for them.

When something is dead and stinking in our own lives and in need of a resurrection, we need to put our faith firmly in the One who said, "I am the resurrection and the life," then proved it over and over. He proved it in the case of Lazarus by raising him from the grave after he had been dead for days, and later when He arose from the dead three days after suffering and dying so that we could have eternal life.

It's an exhilarating, empowering experience when Jesus does a resurrection on our behalf. But what's even more wonderful is the fact that when He raises something from the dead, it leads to even *more* life.

RESURRECTIONS MULTIPLIED

I can only imagine the initial reaction of those at the scene as they saw this body that had been dead four days walking out of the tomb and into the sunlight. At first, some of the people there had to be frightened—startled out of their wits—at seeing what had been a dead man walking. All had to have been in absolute awe at what they were seeing.

But the event was more than sheer spectacle. Something else occurred that day—something with eternal significance. You might call it a chain reaction of life. A miracle raised Lazarus from the dead. And following on the heels of this, an even greater miracle swept through the crowd of previously unbelieving witnesses who saw a man emerge from death into the sunshine of life. "Therefore many of the Jews who came to Mary, and saw what He had done, believed in Him" (John 11:45).

This is an example of one resurrection leading to many more, as many spiritually dead people on the scene were made alive that day. With their own eyes, they saw what Jesus had done, and became convinced in their hearts that He was everything He had claimed to be, that He truly was the "resurrection and the life."

Of course there were some who still couldn't believe Jesus, even though He had responded to the faith of the few and raised a man from the dead. John reports that some of the people on the scene ran back to Jerusalem to tell the Pharisees what Jesus had done. John doesn't tell us the upshot of their reports. It's possible that some may have been moved to believe in Jesus and wanted to tell their spiritual leaders about it. But it's also evident that many who went to the authorities were simply "ratting Jesus out."

The Pharisees, these learned men who had spent their lives studying the Scripture, had somehow missed the One who fulfilled everything the Old Testament had said about the coming Messiah. And when they heard the reports of this miracle, their response was to discuss how to stop Jesus before the entire nation of Israel believed in Him.

When it comes to bringing our hurts, grief, sickness, and confusion to God, we need to understand something. It is only when we demonstrate that we believe Him—and believe that He really cares when we are hurting—that we will see Him raise something from the dead in our lives. Yes, that kind of faith will almost certainly bring us opposition from those who don't believe. But it can also lead to life for those who hear us proclaim the name of Jesus Christ, and watch as God does the miraculous for us.

BELIEF AND OUR LIFE STORY

A good author or screenwriter knows that in order to keep readers' or moviegoers' interest until the very end, he has to keep them in some suspense. There have to be some twists and turns as well as mystery about how the story will finally wrap up. Sometimes that means throwing a few artistic "curveballs" into the story...just to keep us guessing. If the story is done well, you see at the end that the author was in control of the story and had its final outcome mapped out ahead of time.

That is often how God writes the story of our lives. He knows something we don't, and that's how our particular life story will end. Oftentimes He doesn't reveal to us what we need to know about our story until the very last moment...right in the nick of time. He also knows the twists and turns He plans to lead us through, and how they will enhance our story and bring us to a point of believing Him.

No one but Jesus knew how the story of His friend's sickness and physical death would end, including Mary and Martha. But Jesus took the time to teach them the importance of believing Him, and because they heard, believed, and responded, He was able to put the glory of God on display for all of them to see.

God cares when we don't believe, and He will take whatever steps are necessary in order to bring us to a point of believing Him and taking Him at His word. And when we come to that place, we'll have the privilege of seeing God's glory put on display in our own lives as well as in the lives of others around us.

And what will that look like?

It will be a picture of life out of death.

9

God, Do You Really Care...
WHEN I'M TRAPPED?

I've always loved Monopoly.

It's one of my all-time favorite board games. I enjoy the wheeling and dealing and the "hostile takeovers," and there have been nights playing this game when I could do no wrong. On the other hand, I've also had those nights where it seemed like I just couldn't stay out of jail.

If you're familiar with Monopoly, you know that at one corner of every board is the "jail." And you know that if you wind up there, you're trapped! You can't do anything while you're in jail. You can't buy or sell real estate. You can't build houses or hotels. You can't pass "go" and you can't collect $200.

Jail time comes on you suddenly—just when you're on a roll. One moment you're planning a new condo on Park Place, and then in a blink of the eye, you're sent to the slammer. No lawyer, no reading of your rights, no judge, no jury, no trial—just straight to jail with you. This can make for a long night of sitting in your cell and watching other players buy and sell and strengthen their chances of winning the game.

In Monopoly, there are only two ways to get out of jail. You can buy your way out, if you have enough money and if you're willing to spend it, or you can use a "get out jail free" card...if you're lucky enough to draw one when your turn comes. I can remember nights where it seemed I rotted in jail for hours on end—until I finally drew that wonderful, liberating card. *Free at last! Free at last! Thank God Almighty, I am free at last!*

We all know that Monopoly is nothing more than a fun board game we can use to pass the time and enjoy the company of our friends (as well as take them to the cleaners once in a while). But as I've played, it has occurred to me that there is a spiritual application to the game, especially when it comes to "getting out jail free."

Each of us, from birth on, is trapped in a spiritual jail. But it's a jail we can't buy our way out of, and one from which there is no card to release us. Having "the luck of the draw" won't help us. Neither will our skill and experience. We are hopelessly trapped with no way out. I'm referring, of course, to the "jail" of sin, which has us on our way to an eternity apart from God.

But there is Good News! God cares so much that we are trapped in the bondage of sin and death that He did what we could never do: He made a way to give us ultimate and eternal freedom. Our heavenly Father loved us so much that He sent His one and only Son to pay the price for our sin on Calvary's Cross.

In Monopoly terms, He paid for a "Get out of Hell Free" card for each of us, which we get to use when we put our faith in Christ as our Lord and Savior.

It's tremendously freeing to know that God has given us a way to escape His ultimate wrath (hell) and to receive eternal life in His presence (heaven). But there is more to God's kind of freedom than knowing we're on our way to a sweet by-and-by.

The wonderful truth is that God has actually freed us—today, right now—to be everything He intended us to be in the first place. He's freed us so that we can live lives that please Him in every way, and freed us to make a difference for His kingdom.

"UNBIND HIM AND LET HIM GO!"

Have you ever been literally trapped? Maybe stuck in an elevator or locked into a room or someplace you couldn't get out of? If so, you know it can be at the very least frustrating…and sometimes downright frightening.

In the eleventh chapter of John, we've been reading about Lazarus, the object of one of our Lord's most incredible miracles. But even after Jesus raised Lazarus from the dead, the former corpse was *still* literally trapped. He may have been out of the tomb, but he still wasn't completely free.

Let me explain.

After the people in Bethany had done what it took to demonstrate that they believed Him—removed the stone from the grave—and after He prayed, He finally did what He had come to do in the first place.

"Lazarus, come forth," Jesus called out, and that is exactly what happened. This man, whose dead body had been rotting in that dark cave for four full days, shocked everyone on the scene when he got up and walked to the mouth of the tomb. Lazarus truly was alive again. The body that four days earlier had ceased to function now resumed operating as though he had never even been sick, let alone dead.

But Jesus wasn't finished with Lazarus even yet.

John tells us that there was still a problem when it came to Lazarus continuing a normal life: "The man who had died came forth, bound hand and foot in wrappings, and his face was wrapped around with a cloth" (John 11:44).

You see, Lazarus was literally in bondage, tied up head to toe in the burial wrappings the Jewish people traditionally put around the bodies of those who had died. He must have looked like the mummy we've all seen in those old Boris Karloff pictures, except that the mummy in those movies could move his arms and hands and legs freely— and see well enough to chase down the archeologists who had disturbed his sleep.

Even though Lazarus was alive again, in a very real sense death was still holding him down. Yes, he was up and he was out. But he still wasn't free. He could barely move his arms and legs, and he couldn't see a thing. But Jesus was about to finish what He had started. He had given Lazarus new life, but now He would give him freedom as well.

"Unbind him and let him go!"

Moments before, the people at the gravesite had demonstrated a measure of faith by obediently removing the stone that had sealed Lazarus's tomb. When they again obeyed, Lazarus was free from the trappings of death—free to be physically alive and—more than that—to actually live.

In a very real sense, that is what Jesus does for each and every one of us today. Sadly, however, too many of us who have received His gift of eternal life are living our lives here on earth as though we don't know that Jesus has freed us. We aren't talking right, walking right, or moving right, simply because the trappings of death still have us in their grip.

In other words, we're still walking around in our grave clothes.

FREED FOR A PURPOSE

Jesus once told a group of Pharisees who were questioning Him, "The thief comes only to steal and kill and destroy; I came that they may have life, and have it abundantly" (John 10:10). To me, this implies that there is more to knowing Jesus Christ as our Lord and Savior than just waiting around to die so that we can go to heaven. It tells me that Jesus wants to give us a life of freedom, a life that reflects what He's done for us in the eternal sense.

That's a life Jesus wants us to live *here and now.*

But why, if Jesus came to give us abundant life and true freedom, are so many believers more like "dead men walking" than the living, breathing reflections of the life Jesus came to bring? Why are they still tied up and trapped in their problems, in their addictions, in their strongholds? Why are they still bound up in the clothing of death when Jesus has given them life eternal? I believe it's because there are many of us who don't even realize just how free they really are.

But that can change. Maybe even today.

THE EXPERIENCE OF FREEDOM

On June 19, those of us who live in the great state of Texas celebrate a holiday we call "Juneteenth," which commemorates the final granting of freedom to slaves in this state on that date in 1865.

If you're familiar with United States history, you may know that President Abraham Lincoln's Emancipation Proclamation went into effect on January 1, 1863, which meant that all slaves in the rebel states were legally free. After the end of the Civil War and the defeat of the South, slavery should have ended in all states. But that didn't happen in Texas until June 19, 1865, when Union General Gordon Granger rode into Galveston and read General Order #3, which began, "The people of Texas are informed that, in accordance with a proclamation from the Executive of the United States, all slaves are free."

At that point, former slaves all over Texas started packing their bags and heading out for other states, hoping to make better lives for themselves as free men and women.

As far as federal law was concerned, the slaves in Texas had been legally freed on January 1, 1863. But as far as actually *experiencing* that freedom, it took another two and one half years.

Why did it take so long? Because during the Civil War, the Union armies never successfully invaded Texas, and the practice of slavery continued to flourish. In fact, many slave-owners from other states came to Texas and brought their slaves with them to wait out the war, hoping that the Confederacy would win. Wealthy, powerful, and influential, Texas slaveholders were able to squelch and suppress the news of the Emancipation.

This piece of Texas history demonstrates something we as Christians need to understand. Freedom doesn't mean anything unless we know we are free and can actually enjoy and live in that freedom.

People in power throughout history have used religion to keep the masses trapped and in bondage. But Jesus Himself repeatedly stated to everyone who had ears to hear that His mission on earth was to bring freedom to those who placed their faith in Him.

JESUS' MISSION OF FREEDOM

Jesus spent the entirety of His earthly ministry knowing that He was the Promised One, the Messiah spoken of in the Old Testament. Early in that ministry, Jesus traveled to His hometown of Nazareth, where He attended the local synagogue. When the leaders gave Him the scroll of the prophet Isaiah—a prophecy written hundreds of years back in Israel's history—he read these words to those who assembled that day: "The Spirit of the Lord is on me, because he has anointed me to preach good news to the poor. *He has sent me to proclaim freedom for the prisoners* and recovery of sight for the blind, *to release the oppressed*, to proclaim the year of the Lord's favor" (Luke 4:18–19, NIV).

The simple reading of that passage didn't raise any eyebrows; they'd heard those words many times before. But moments later, Jesus rocked them back on their heels with something they had never heard before.

"Today this Scripture has been fulfilled in your hearing" (Luke 4:21).

In other words, Jesus was telling the crowd, "You've been waiting for your Messiah and looking forward to the freedom He is coming to bring you. Well, you're looking at Him right now. I am that Messiah."

Later, Jesus taught at the Temple in Jerusalem, where many of the Jewish people responded to His message and believed in Him. Part of that message was a clear declaration of freedom—an emancipation proclamation—through faith in Him.

> So Jesus was saying to those Jews who had believed Him, "If you continue in My word, then you are truly disciples of Mine; and you will know the truth, and the truth will make you free." They answered Him, "We are Abraham's descendants and have never yet been enslaved to anyone; how is it that You say, 'You will become free'?" Jesus answered them, "Truly, truly, I say to you, everyone who commits sin is the slave of sin. The slave does not remain in the house forever; the son does remain forever. So if the Son makes you free, you will be free indeed."
>
> JOHN 8:31–36

Free indeed! Difficult as this message may have been for the Jewish leadership to swallow, it's a theme that rings loud and clear through the pages of the New Testament. It was part and parcel of the Good News Jesus had called men and women to take into the world after He was gone.

THE LOOK OF FREEDOM IN CHRIST

Probably the most important and influential of the messengers Jesus sent out was the apostle Paul, who spoke a great deal about our freedom in Christ. Paul wrote that in Christ we have been freed...

- *from the bondage of sin*: "But thanks be to God that though you were slaves of sin, you became obedient from the heart to that form of teaching to which you were committed, and having been freed from sin, you became slaves of righteousness" (Romans 6:17–18);
- *from spiritual death*: "For the wages of sin is death, but the free gift of God is eternal life in Christ Jesus our Lord" (Romans 6:23);
- *from bondage to the law*: "Therefore, my brethren, you also were made to die to the Law through the body of Christ, so that you might be joined to another, to Him who was raised from the dead, in order that we might bear fruit for God. For while we were in the flesh, the sinful passions,

which were aroused by the Law, were at work in the members of our body to bear fruit for death. But now we have been released from the Law, having died to that by which we were bound, so that we serve in newness of the Spirit and not in oldness of the letter" (Romans 7:4–6);

- *from the guilt and condemnation of sin*: "Therefore there is now no condemnation for those who are in Christ Jesus" (Romans 8:1);

- *from the power of sin and death*: "The sting of death is sin, and the power of sin is the law; but thanks be to God, who gives us the victory through our Lord Jesus Christ" (1 Corinthians 15:56–57);

- *from human regulations*: "But it was because of the false brethren secretly brought in, who had sneaked in to spy out our liberty which we have in Christ Jesus, in order to bring us into bondage. But we did not yield in subjection to them for even an hour, so that the truth of the gospel would remain with you" (Galatians 2:4–5);

- *from the enemy's false accusations*: "Once you were alienated from God and were enemies in your minds because of your evil behavior. But now he has reconciled you by Christ's physical body through death to present you holy in his sight, without blemish and free from accusation" (Colossians 1:21–22, NIV).

The Bible makes it clear that Jesus came to bring freedom to those who would by faith know Him as their Lord and Savior. Why, then, don't we live that way? Why do so many of us live out our days like hostages? Even those of us who know what the Bible says about our freedom in Jesus Christ, still find ourselves trapped and shackled by sin, guilt, doubt, our past, and anything else the devil wants to throw in our pathway to trip us up. If the evil one can't take us to hell, he can still squeeze the joy out of our lives here on earth, and keep us from walking in the kind of freedom Paul wrote about and Jesus came to give us.

When we first come to Jesus Christ in faith, we are given eternal life and our destiny in heaven with Him is sealed. Eternal life—life at a higher level—begins the moment you say yes to Christ. But some of us are still walking around in grave clothes, dragging around the trappings of death wherever we go. That is literally what Lazarus did when he first came out of the grave, and it is spiritually what so many of us do even after we've been saved.

But there is something we need to catch when it comes to receiving new life and then walking in that life. When Jesus raised Lazarus from the dead, He still had more work to do: the relatively minor task of removing the trappings of death. Trashing the old shroud. It would only be after these trappings were removed that Lazarus would be completely free to resume his life as a friend and follower of Jesus.

Before someone accepts Jesus Christ as Savior, he or she is spiritually dead in trespasses and sin and well on the way to eternal separation from God. But upon conversion, something miraculous happens: That person is made *spiritually* alive, just as Lazarus was made *physically* alive the moment Jesus called him out of the tomb.

What I want you to think about is this: If Jesus could raise what was absolutely dead and stinking to life, how much more is He able to remove the trappings of death so that the one who was once dead can start living—really living—the life He has for us!

Living a life of faith means knowing that Jesus has given us freedom from the wardrobe of the tomb. And never forget that this mighty release has an impact both in eternity and in the right-here-and-now. He has released us from the chains of sin and death and given us eternal life in heaven, and He has set us free from everything that keeps us from living a life that pleases God.

Knowing we are free in Christ motivates and empowers us to be the kind of Christ-followers who make a difference in the world around us, the kind who give freely out of the freedom we have received.

FREE TO FREE ONE ANOTHER

If you've ever seen someone in a straightjacket, you know that (unless you're Harry Houdini) it's nearly impossible for him or her to escape without help. With the hands and arms tethered down in the jacket, the average person just can't break free. In the physical sense, that person is trapped and in bondage.

That's not unlike Lazarus's situation when he first stepped out of the dark mouth of that tomb. John tells us that he was "bound hand and foot with wrappings." That must have meant he was barely able to make his way out of that cave and into the sunlight, let alone walk, talk, and see freely. Obviously, Lazarus was bound so tightly and so head-to-toe that he needed to be set free from his "burial suit."

Earlier, I pointed out how Jesus gave the people at Lazarus's tomb the opportunity to demonstrate that they believed Him with the command, "Remove the stone." He followed that command with "Unwrap him and let him go."

There's a principle in Jesus' commands that day, and it is this: God wants to use those of us He has already freed to help free others. The Gospel of Matthew tells us that after the disciples had spent time with Jesus listening to His teaching and observing His miracles, He sent them out on their first "missionary journey" with these marching orders: "Heal the sick, raise the dead, cleanse the lepers, cast out demons. Freely you received, freely give" (Matthew 10:8).

Earlier in this chapter, I listed some of the things the apostle Paul tells us Jesus frees us *from*—most importantly the power of sin and spiritual death. But Paul also tells us throughout his letters that we are also freed *for* certain actions and privileges. Because we know Jesus Christ as our Lord and Savior, there are things we *get* to do freely in His name:

- *Serve Christ.* "For he who was called in the Lord while a slave, is the Lord's freedman; likewise he who was called while free, is Christ's slave" (1 Corinthians 7:22).
- *Serve others in the name of Christ.* "For though I am free from all men, I have made myself a slave to all, so that I may win more" (1 Corinthians 9:19).
- *Seek only God's best for others.* "All things are lawful, but not all things are profitable. All things are lawful, but not all things edify. Let no one seek his own good, but that of his neighbor" (1 Corinthians 10:23–24).
- *Serve one another in love.* "For you were called to freedom, brethren; only do not turn your freedom into an opportunity for the flesh, but through love serve one another" (Galatians 5:13).
- *Approach our heavenly Father confidently.* "In him and through faith in him we may approach God with freedom and confidence" (Ephesians 3:12, NIV).

Did you notice? Many of the things the Bible says we are free to do involve "doing" for others in the name of Jesus. When He said, "Freely you have received, freely give," it was a command. He never intended for us to hoard our blessings or take our freedom for granted.

If God has made you spiritually alive through your faith in Jesus Christ, then "unwrapped" you from the trappings of death, you'll be ready to help out when someone else needs to be freed. And you won't have to look very far...open your eyes and you will see people staggering around in grave clothes all around you.

How do you help free people from the trappings of death? It begins as you express your willingness to God, and allow the Holy Spirit to show you what to do and to bring needy people across your path. For example, if He has delivered you from a specific sin, habit, or addiction, you may have the opportunity to help free someone else who is still tied up in the same thing. If He has freed you to enjoy a strong and happy marriage, then you may have a chance to help out someone else whose marriage is struggling.

But how do you find those opportunities to help lead others into the full freedom Jesus came to bring them? It starts by taking the time to build intimacy with Him, something anyone who has been freed from death and its entanglements will be motivated to do.

FROM THE TOMB TO THE TABLE

John records an interesting and very telling scene a short time after Jesus raised Lazarus from the dead. It's a clear demonstration of what happens when Jesus gives us life then releases us from our cemetery outfits: "Jesus, therefore, six days before the Passover, came to Bethany where Lazarus was, whom Jesus had raised from the dead. So they made Him a supper there, and Martha was serving; but Lazarus was one of those reclining at the table with Him" (John 12:1–2).

Here's an interesting contrast between two expressions of love for Jesus. While Martha was busy being a hostess and showing Jesus and the others some hospitality, Lazarus was "reclining at the table with Him." In the Bible, when we read the word *reclining*, we can know that it usually refers to spending time breaking bread with someone, with fellowshipping and building intimacy with that person.

Those of us who are happily married understand the difference between expressing our love through acts of service (doing different tasks for one another) and expressing it by doing and saying the things that build real intimacy. For example, if I get up bright and early on a Saturday morning and go outside and wash my wife's car inside and out, I've expressed my love for her through something I've done. But I know that simply washing her car—while it may put a smile on her face because she doesn't have to drive around in a dirty automobile—doesn't build intimacy between us. That can only happen as I spend time with her and talk with her and ask questions to find out what's on her heart and share with her what's on my own heart.

While we shouldn't be critical of Martha for doing the "leg-work" of serving Jesus and the others at the dinner in Bethany, we should pay special attention to how Lazarus responded to the miracle Jesus had done for him. Jesus had just given Lazarus life and also made sure that He was freed from the trappings of death. As a result, Lazarus was pursuing a deeper relationship with the Lord. Already a good friend of Jesus, he now wanted that friendship to be more close and intimate than ever.

What would you think of this man Lazarus if he had shrugged away his resurrection, and said it wasn't a big deal? What would you think if he acted as though he had never been freed from death and its trappings? What if he took a casual, nonchalant attitude toward Jesus, and pushed the friendship to one side? We would say, "What an ungrateful lout! What's wrong with that man?"

But isn't that how we respond to our Lord when we take our eternal salvation for granted, accept our promised freedom with a yawn, and neglect our relationship with Him? How can we be "casual" with the One who has called us out of darkness and death and released us from its putrid wrappings?

When Jesus raises you from the dead and in the spiritual sense then "unwraps" you from the trappings of death, your heart should leap toward intimacy with Him. When you think of what He has done for you, how could you not want to be with Him, and enjoy His friendship? As with Lazarus, you will want to "recline with Him at the table" always, and learn more about Him and His heart's desire for you.

FREEDOM FROM FEAR

As I said earlier, death is probably man's greatest fear. People are afraid to die, and afraid of having their loved ones die.

John tells us that, humanly speaking, Lazarus had something to fear from Jesus' enemies. There was a death threat on the resurrected man's head.

> Meanwhile a large crowd of Jews found out that Jesus was there and came, not only because of him but also to see Lazarus, whom he had raised from the dead. So the chief priests made plans to kill Lazarus as well, for on account of him many of the Jews were going over to Jesus and putting their faith in him.
>
> JOHN 12:9-11, NIV

The news of Lazarus's resurrection made its way around the Jerusalem area very quickly, and some of the people who had heard about it were none too pleased. These were the chief priests and Jewish religious leaders who now not only wanted Jesus put to death, they wanted to kill Lazarus, too. *That,* they reasoned, would put a stop to all this talk about resurrection. Why would they do such a thing? Because what Jesus had done for Lazarus had led many of the Jews to believe in Him. And that just couldn't be tolerated.

This is the only time in history that I know of where a man who had already died was threatened with death, and it happened for one reason: Lazarus's new life was bringing attention to the Lord Jesus Christ.

John doesn't tell us how Lazarus responded to the news that the religious establishment of that time wanted him dead—or whether he responded at all—but I can't help but think that it didn't bother or frighten him all that much. After all, he had *already* been dead! He knew that there was nothing they could do to him that Jesus couldn't handle. And maybe he also knew something that few men in history could ever know...that death wasn't such a bad prospect after all.

The Bible doesn't tell us anything about Lazarus's life or faith before his death and resurrection. But we can see from reading what he did after he had been raised from the dead that he didn't stress about threats to his life. How do we know this? Because he obviously wasn't afraid or ashamed to spend time with Jesus and to be identified as one His followers.

Lazarus's "new" life principle was that nothing—not even threats to his life—was going to keep him from associating freely and openly with the One who not only gave him new life but who also freed him from the trappings of death.

The question each of us who believes in Jesus Christ must ask is this: *Who is coming to Jesus because of me?* Each of us who knows Jesus as our Lord and Savior has been called and made alive in Him.

And we've also been "unwrapped" or liberated from the accessories of death, freeing us from the power of sin and death to be a testimony for Him.

God cares when we are trapped. How much does He care? No one on earth could ever calculate it. He cares so much that He sent His Son to free us from the power of darkness, both here on earth and in the eternity to come. And when Jesus makes us "free indeed," we can respond in no other way than to draw nearer to Him, so near that people around us see our identification with Him.

When that happens, others will be drawn to Jesus and to the freedom He offers in such wonderful abundance.

10

OH YES, HE CARES!

If ever a group of people needed the message "God cares," it was the first-century believers in the fledgling church in Jerusalem.

Christians in that time and place faced fierce opposition from both the Jewish religious establishment and the Roman government. Within decades following the establishment of the church, Rome had adopted an official policy of persecution of Christians. Because of that, these believers faced rejection from their friends, family, and fellow countrymen, the confiscation of their land and other personal property, and even imprisonment and death.

All because they believed in and served Jesus Christ.

Many of these believers became so deeply discouraged that they were close to throwing in the towel, abandoning their faith altogether. They, like Mary and Martha when Jesus first arrived on the outskirts of Bethany, had to be wondering where He was or whether He really cared that they were suffering.

Nothing will shake a believer's faith like believing the devil's lie that Jesus doesn't really care when His people suffer—or that if He does care, there's really nothing He can do about it. But in the midst of all this persecution, suffering, and discouragement a letter of encouragement arrived…a letter we've come to know as the New Testament book of Hebrews.

The writer, unknown to us today, assured these stressed, suffering people that Jesus cared very much about what they were enduring, and that He was there for them to give them what they needed to hold on.

One of the most encouraging passages in the entire Bible is found in Hebrews 4. In it, the writer assures believers that Jesus not only cares when we're facing tough times, but that He takes action on our behalf in the very midst of them:

Therefore, since we have a great high priest who has passed through the heavens, Jesus the Son of God, let us hold fast to our confession. For we do not have a high priest who cannot sympathize with our weaknesses, but One who has been tempted in all things as we are, yet without sin. Therefore, let us draw near with confidence to the throne of grace, so that we may receive mercy and find grace to help in time of need.

HEBREWS 4:14—16

This passage (a great one to memorize!) contains one of the most encouraging promises in all of Scripture regarding God's care for us in times of crisis. It is rich in little tidbits all believers can apply to their lives anytime, but especially when they are hurting. But in order to fully grasp it and personalize it, we need to understand some things about the language and images it uses as it encouraged those suffering Jewish believers nearly two thousand years ago.

THE *GREAT* HIGH PRIEST

Most Christians today really can't grasp the role of the first-century high priest. And yet this was an understanding deeply woven into the culture and religious lives of devout first-century Jews in the days of the early church.

Jewish people knew the high priest as the mediator or representative between the ordinary, average person and a holy God. They knew the high priest as the one responsible for presenting sacrifices to God on the annual Day of Atonement so that their sins could be covered for the whole year.

The main theme of the book of Hebrews is the high priesthood of the Lord Jesus Christ. The writer of this letter refers to Him as "a merciful and faithful high priest in service to God...that he might make atonement for the sins of the people" (2:17, NIV) and as "the apostle and high priest whom we confess" (3:1, NIV).

Hebrews identifies Jesus as the New Covenant replacement for the human high priesthood, which God had put in place temporarily and as a forerunner to the ultimate once-and-for-all sacrifice of Jesus Christ, the eternal Son of God, on the Cross. It showed early Jewish Christians that Jesus fulfilled every requirement God had for the forgiveness of sins and the redemption of humankind.

Obviously, the office of high priest was incredibly important to the Jews. The high priest wasn't elected by the people but was chosen by God Himself, and the responsibilities of the office were awesome. But the writer of Hebrews goes to great lengths to explain the superiority of Jesus over a sacrificial system that employed a human high priest. He refers to Jesus as a *"great* high priest," identifies Him by His human name—Jesus Christ—then by His eternal title—the Son of God.

Let's stop for just a minute of focus. God wants us to understand the uniqueness of Jesus. He wants us to understand that Jesus was fully human like us, meaning that He experienced the same things we experience daily here on earth, but that He was also completely unlike us as the only begotten Son of God.

Every other Jewish priest up to that point—including the high priest—was a man and nothing more. High priests held a high and vitally important office, but being human, they had the same limitations each and every one of us has. They were representatives between humans and God, but they were finite beings, meaning they all died and went on to their eternal rewards.

Jesus, on the other hand, was different from the human high priests because as the Son of God, He not only was a mediator between God and humanity but He was also deity. That is the very same message the apostle Paul's letter to the Colossians gives us when it reads, "in Him all the fullness of Deity dwells in bodily form" (2:9).

A HEAVENLY HIGH PRIEST

Hebrews 4:14 not only identifies Jesus as the Son of God, but it also tells us something else we might find easy to overlook: Jesus the great high priest "passed through the heavens."

When the Bible uses the word *heaven*, it is speaking of one of three different realms. First, there is the atmospheric heaven, the one that surrounds the earth and contains oxygen, clouds, water, and other natural elements. Second, there are the stellar heavens, the physical universe that includes planets, stars, galaxies, and every other celestial body. Finally there is the heaven where God Himself sits on His throne.

But what does it mean to us that Jesus passed through these heavens? It's a big, awesome message, one the Jewish readers of this letter would understand, and one we as modern-day gentile Christians also need to grasp.

As I pointed out earlier, in Old Testament times the Jewish high priest was solely responsible for performing the sacrifices during the annual Day of Atonement. It was on this day that the high priest entered into the tabernacle by passing through the outer court, walking through the inner court, then into the very presence of God. There in the Holy of Holies, he sprinkled blood on the mercy seat—the act that made it possible for God to forgive the sins of His people for another year.

When the writer of Hebrews spoke of the "great high priest who has passed through the heavens," he was using a word picture Jewish readers would have immediately understood. What it declared was Jesus' presence in all three parts of the temple: the outer court, the inner court, and, of course, the presence of God Himself in the holiest of holies.

Jesus our High Priest has passed through all three heavenly realms. He spent thirty-three years walking, talking, teaching, preaching, and healing on earth. And when His mission on earth was complete, He left the realm of earthly time and went back into eternity, back into the very presence of God the Father, where He represents us before Him. And while the best an earthly high priest could do was to represent the people before God once a year, on the

Day of Atonement, our High Priest sits at the right hand of God, pleading our case 24/7!

So what is the writer of Hebrews telling us is so special about our High Priest? Simply that He gives us something all of us need if we are to find eternal life: Access to God Himself.

ACCESS TO THE FATHER

There's a story (one I am told is true, or at least based in fact) of a soldier sitting on a park bench in Washington D.C. at some point during the Civil War. The man was obviously distraught, and when a small boy happened by the bench he noticed that this soldier was weeping.

"What's wrong, sir?" the lad asked, and the soldier told him that he desperately needed to see President Abraham Lincoln but had been denied access to the president's office. "Take my hand and follow me," the little boy offered, then led the soldier up to gate of the president's mansion, past the guards, and into the mansion itself. The boy then led the soldier into the office of Abraham Lincoln himself.

"Father," the boy said, "this soldier needs to talk to you."

There's something very empowering about knowing the son of a person of power, isn't there? And that is our position and unspeakable privilege as those who know Jesus Christ as Lord and Savior.

Because we know the One who sits at the right hand of the Father, who has His ear, and who receives everything He asks of the Father, we have access to the Father Himself.

In Old Testament times, the people had access to God through the human high priest—but with strict and severe limitations. Under the Old Covenant, you couldn't just walk into the presence of God without the high priest, and even that access was limited and temporary. The high priest himself couldn't enter the Holy of Holies more than once a year, and even when he did enter he couldn't stay long. But under the New Covenant, we have constant, uninterrupted access to God, simply because our High Priest, Jesus Christ, is at His right hand always.

Having that kind of amazing, incomprehensible right of entry, the writer tells us, is the very reason we should remain confident and steadfast in our faith—even in the face of heartbreak, pain, and trials. "Therefore, since we have a great high priest who has passed through the heavens, Jesus the Son of God, *let us hold fast our confession*" (Hebrews 4:14).

In other words, Hebrews was telling those first-century Jewish believers, *don't quit!* Don't turn away from your faith in Jesus Christ simply because you are persecuted and suffering. Hold on to your confidence, because you have been granted entry into the presence of the very Creator of the universe, because you know His Son.

Still, I can't help but wonder. Many of these first-century Jewish Christians faced persecution more horrible than any we today can imagine. Might these beaten-down, discouraged souls have read the writer's encouragement to hold fast to their faith with a rather jaundiced view? Yes, it was nice to have a little "pep talk," but they must have wondered the same thing many believers today still wonder when they endure difficult or painful times: Where is Jesus *right now*?

Maybe you've asked that question just lately. Perhaps even today.

You want and need to know where God is when you are sick, when you are grieving, when you are suffering, and when you don't really know for sure that He even cares about your personal situation.

There's an answer to those kinds of questions. It's simple, it's wonderful, and it's right in the very portion of Scripture we've been looking at.

WITH US

We know by faith that God is in His heaven and that He demonstrates a measure of control over everything that happens down here on earth. But as we wrestle with our problems day by day, we begin to think of God as "far away" and wonder if He really cares about our personal lives.

The writer of Hebrews encourages us to "hold fast to our confession," or, as another version of the Bible puts it, "never stop trusting him" (4:14, NLT). But this passage gives us further encouragement, telling us, "We do not have a high priest who cannot sympathize with our weaknesses, but One who has been tempted in all things as we are, yet without sin" (Hebrews 4:15).

It's important to focus closely on the wording of this verse because it tells us something very, very important we need to know about our relationship with Jesus. *He understands what we're going through because He's been there Himself.*

The writer of Hebrews uses the word *sympathize,* which carries with it the idea of actually suffering with someone who hurts, even to the point of feeling what they feel. It's one thing to listen to someone pour out their hurts, understand how they feel, and even grieve for them. But it's a whole other level of caring when we personally enter into their pain and grieve *with* them.

But what best qualifies someone to actually sympathize with someone in need and pain? Simply having experienced the same things they have experienced. For example, someone who has endured the pain of losing a loved one or of going through a divorce is better equipped to sympathize with someone who has just faced those same devastations.

As the old saying goes, "You have to walk a mile in their shoes."

That, friends, is exactly what Jesus did when He left His Father in heaven, came to earth and spent thirty-three years living among humans in human form.

Jesus is infinitely superior to any earthly high priest because

He's not limited to mere human understanding when it comes to our pain and weakness. While an earthly priest could give you words of comfort and some understanding, Jesus has given Himself to actually feeling anything and everything we feel.

Our God is infinite in His knowledge and wisdom, but there are some things He had limited Himself from doing, one of which was knowing what it was like to be human, to feel the emotions we feel and to endure the pain we endure. That is why He couldn't have just finished the act of redemption from heaven, but instead had to come to earth as a man. He wanted to see *everything* we see, hear *everything* we hear, and feel *everything* we feel.

Living in a fallen world, many of us know what it feels like to

...be attacked by the devil;

...be tempted;

...be hungry and thirsty;

...grieve over the death of a loved one;

...be rejected by your own people;

...be unfairly criticized, scorned, and talked about;

...be verbally chastised and threatened for speaking the truth;

...be punished and abused when you've done nothing to deserve it;

...be unfairly charged and wrongly convicted;

...have your closest friends turn their backs on you in your hour of need;

...face death, even a slow and excruciatingly painful death.

While all of us have felt the pain of *some*, or maybe even *most*, of the things I've listed above, not all of us have dealt with *all* those situations personally. Not so with Jesus. During the course of His life on earth, there is nothing in that list that Jesus didn't endure.

Not one thing!

But there was more. Jesus was like those of us who live in a fallen, sinful world in that it was sin that ultimately did Him in. Jesus personally experienced the penalty for sin, which is death. The difference between Him and us in that respect, however, is that it wasn't *His* sin—because He was without sin—but our sin that led to His death on the Cross.

So...if Jesus was without sin, how can He understand me, a sinful creature, and my weaknesses?

The apostle Paul wrote, "He made Him who knew no sin to be sin on our behalf, so that we might become the righteousness of God in Him" (2 Corinthians 5:21). This tells us that while Jesus lived a life of sinless perfection, He still knew how it felt to be separated from His Father because of sin.

When Jesus went to the Cross, He went as the ultimate blood sacrifice for our sins. The Bible tells us that "without shedding of blood, there is no forgiveness [of sins]" (Hebrews 9:22). From the very beginning, God required that humankind's sins be paid for with the shedding of blood. In the Old Testament, there were various blood sacrifices for the remission of sin, all of which were forerunners of the ultimate sacrifice: Jesus' death on the Cross.

As Jesus hung bleeding and dying on the Cross, He took on Himself every sin that had been committed or ever would be committed. At that moment, the Father and the Son felt the horror of the first-ever and never-to-be-repeated break of their eternally perfect relationship. As Jesus became sin on the Cross for us, He cried out, "My God, My God, why have You forsaken Me?" (Mark 15:34) For the first time in all of eternity past, His Father couldn't even look at Him.

That was the next to last human experience Jesus faced. Moments later, He experienced what each and every one of us will one day face.

Physical death.

At that point, Jesus had endured everything we as humans have to endure on this side of the kingdom. He had indeed "walked a mile in our shoes."

PERFECT SYMPATHY

When we take our pain, confusion, and weaknesses to Jesus, we aren't taking them to someone who just hears and understands (as important as that is) but to Someone who actually *feels* our pain with and for us, someone who fully understands and sympathizes with our every human weakness.

In this context, a weakness is anything that shows our limitations as humans. Each and every one of us has weaknesses, no matter how devoted we are to our relationship with God. These weaknesses can show up in how we think, in how we deal with life's circumstances, in how we are tempted, and in the sins we are most prone to committing.

This is the distinction the writer of Hebrews makes between a human high priest and the Great High Priest, Jesus Christ. In Him, we have a High Priest who is the perfect combination of humanity and deity. He is able to feel our pain and sympathize with our weaknesses, because He's been there. But He can also endure much more than we can and never be broken. He proved that by living the one sinless life ever lived on Planet Earth.

Because Jesus was "tempted in all things but was without sin," He can identify and sympathize with the failings of our weak flesh. But again, that brings up some very important questions. Why, for example, does God allow us to continue living with our weaknesses? Why doesn't He just reach down and give us the sinless perfection of Jesus Christ the minute we come to Him for salvation?

The answer to those questions lies in the kind of relationship God wants us to have with Himself in this life. It's a relationship of complete dependence on Him, a relationship in which we know that without Him we are completely at the mercy of our own human weakness.

You see, God knows that when we feel strong, we are more likely to forget our need for Him and less likely to draw near. On the other hand, He knows that when we feel weak we are more likely to come near to Him with open hands, seeking His sympathy, mercy, and strength.

Those of us who are physically healthy know that we're not likely to see a doctor unless something in our bodies changes, unless we see some kind of problem or troubling symptoms. When we get sick, we'll first try every over-the-counter remedy we can find, but when those don't work, we know it's time to "draw near" the doctor's office.

There's an old saying that goes, "The Lord helps those who help themselves." But as with many old sayings, nothing could be further from the truth. God loves more than anything to bless and strengthen those who acknowledge their own weakness and need.

This is the very point Jesus made to a group of Pharisees. These were men who believed themselves spiritually healthy with no need of Jesus. "It is not those who are healthy who need a physician," Jesus told them, "but those who are sick" (Matthew 9:12).

The writer of Hebrews tells us that Jesus is our High Priest who sympathizes with our weaknesses and helps us when we do one thing: draw near to the throne of grace.

CONFIDENT WEAKNESS

All of us humans have weaknesses.

Notice that in the passage we've been looking at it doesn't say that Jesus sympathizes with us *if* we have weakness. It just assumes that we all have them. And we have a High Priest who cares about them.

The good news for us, however, appears one verse later: "Therefore let us draw near *with confidence* to the throne of grace, so that we may receive mercy and find grace to help in time of need" (Hebrews 4:16).

This verse describes what I call approaching God from a position of "confident weakness." First, we have in Jesus a High Priest who sympathizes with our weaknesses. Second, we have been invited to approach Him, acknowledging our need. But third, and perhaps most importantly, it means we approach Him with confidence, knowing that He wants more than anything to give us sympathy, grace, mercy, and help in our time of need.

Is there a condition to receiving this help from God?

Yes, there is.

And it's found in understanding what the throne of grace really is, and who occupies it.

WHO'S ON THE THRONE?

The book of Hebrews opens with a word picture of Jesus sitting at the right hand of His Father, whom He had served faithfully every moment of His life on earth: "And He is the radiance of His glory and the exact representation of His nature, and upholds all things by the word of His power. When He had made purification of sins, He sat down at the right hand of the Majesty on high" (Hebrews 1:3).

When we approach our heavenly Father, we need to remember that we are approaching the One who sits on the throne, the One who is in charge, and the One who decides everything that happens in our lives. This means that while Jesus sympathizes with us in our weakness, it is the Father who chooses how to help us in those weaknesses.

Those of us who are parents know there are times when we feel sorry about what our children are going through—while at the same time making decisions that are contrary to what the child wants or thinks he needs. We may have the ability and the means to do what the child wants, but we also know that doing so wouldn't be in the best interests of the child.

When a parent sees his child's pain and doesn't intervene in the situation the way the child wants, it doesn't mean that the parent doesn't sympathize. It also doesn't mean we don't have the child's very best in mind.

The very same thing is true with our heavenly Father.

There isn't a believer around who hasn't during a time of weakness pleaded with God to step into a situation and intervene in a specific way—only to find that He wouldn't do it. But that didn't mean that God didn't care, only that He was acting both for His own glory and for the best for His child.

Right about now, you're probably asking, "What good is God's sympathy if He's not doing for me what I hope for and desire?" That's an excellent question, but the truth is that when we approach God's throne, we will always get something, even if it's not what we think we need.

It's called *grace*.

But what exactly is grace? It's simply God doing for us what we can't do for ourselves. It's God supplying us with what we need—even if it's not what we want or *think* we need—until He steps in and changes our situation.

Unfortunately, a lot of us want to dictate to the throne of God during our times of want. Too many have been influenced by the "name it and claim it" preachers out there, who teach that God is somehow obliged to do for us what we say and how we say to do it, simply because we're one of the King's kids.

God will always allow us as His children to approach the throne of grace with confidence and He will always sympathize with us, but He will never let us dictate how He's going to handle the situations we bring before Him. God will always be God, and He will never share His sovereignty with anyone.

Think back about the beginning of the story of Lazarus, a man "Jesus loved." Mary and Martha had summoned Jesus to come and heal their brother, but Jesus waited… waited until God's appointed time to go…waited until Lazarus had died…waited until He had the perfect opportunity to teach everyone involved some lessons about faith.

From the very beginning, Jesus had fully intended to travel to Bethany to do a miracle on His dear friends' behalf. But He would only do that after He had accomplished a higher purpose in the hearts of everyone involved.

BUT WHEN WILL HE ACT?

Hebrews 4:15–16 contains one of the greatest promises in the Bible, which is that God will not only sympathize with us in our weaknesses, but that He will also freely dispense the mercy, grace, and help we need to endure.

But still, you may be asking, "When is God going to step in and resolve my situation?"

Well, I can't tell you that. As a minister of the gospel of Jesus Christ, I am obligated to preach and teach biblical truth, and the truth is that there are times when we can't know when God will intervene and change our situations. And to take that a step further, I have to tell you that there will be times when He *won't* change our situations.

But there is one thing I can tell you with certainty, and it's this: While you are in a place of weakness, pain, grief, trouble, or loss, He will sustain you. He will give you all the grace, mercy, and help you need to get through even the most difficult situations that come your way.

One of the Psalms begins with a great description of this kind of help:

> God is our refuge and strength,
>   A very present help in trouble.
> Therefore we will not fear, though the earth should change
>   And though the mountains slip into the heart of the sea;
> Though its waters roar and foam,
>   Though the mountains quake at its swelling pride.

> PSALM 46:1–3

Note that the psalmist doesn't say that there won't be trouble for those of us who know God, nor does he say God will necessarily deliver us out of trouble right away when we call on Him. In fact, after assuring us that God will be with us and help us in our time of trouble, he then goes on to list huge earthshaking calamities!

It's human nature to want God to step in and change things during our seasons of trouble. We want that kind of help the very minute we call on Him. But the old saying, "Prayer changes *things*" isn't always true. When we step up to the throne of grace, there will be times when God changes our situation, but there will also be times when He allows us to continue in our weakness and difficulty.

Either way, He will put action behind His sympathy. He's won't just say, "I care when you are weak or hurting, and I hope you get through it." God cares more than we can comprehend when we are in the middle of difficult times, and we can rest in His ironclad promise that He will give us the help we need to endure.

Oh yes, He cares, and He has given us a private place to meet with Him when we need His help. It's called His throne of grace, and we can bring anything big or small to Him knowing that the very least He's going to do is give us the help we need to not only endure but to grow and thrive in our faith.

That, my friend, shows us just how very much He cares!

Enjoy these other titles from
Tony Evans

God Can Not Be Trusted (And
Five Other Lies of Satan)
1-59052-417-9

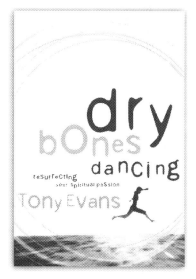

Dry Bones Dancing
1-59052-391-1

The Fire That Ignites
1-59052-083-1

God Is More than Enough
1-59052-337-7

BIG CHANGE

For a complete list of Big Change titles, visit our website at www.bigchangemoments.com

SMALL BOOKS
BIG CHANGE®

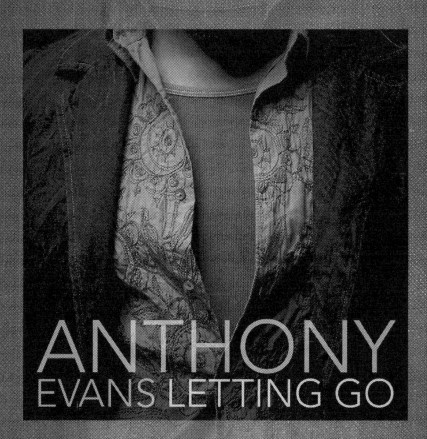

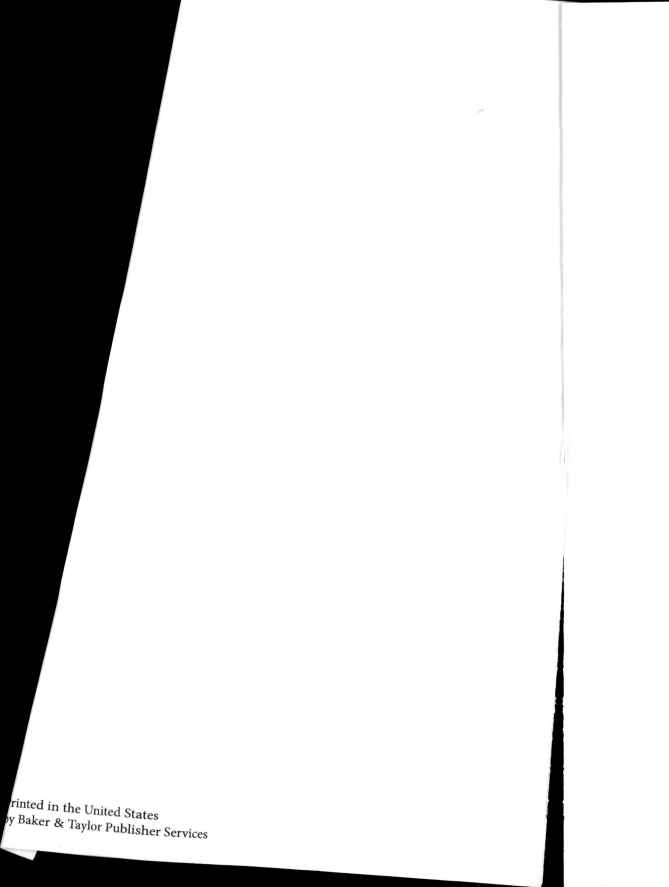

Printed in the United States
by Baker & Taylor Publisher Services